C000062073

WOMEN POETS OF THE NINETEENTH CENTURY

WOMEN POETS OF THE NINETEENTH CENTURY

Emma Mason

© Copyright 2006 by Emma Mason

First published in 2006 by Northcote House Publishers Ltd, Horndon, Tavistock, Devon, PL19 9NQ, United Kingdom.
Tel: +44 (01822) 810066. Fax: +44 (01822) 810034.

British Library Cataloguing-in-Publication Data
A catalogue record for this book is available from the British Library

ISBN 0-7463-1113-3 hardcover
ISBN 0-7463-1001-3 paperback

Typeset by TW Typesetting, Plymouth, Devon
Printed and bound in the United Kingdom by
Athenaeum Press Ltd., Gateshead, Tyne & Wear

Contents

Acknowledgements

Thanks to Isobel Armstrong, Ellen Jordan, Rebecca Lemon, Jon Mee, Jon Roberts, Jason Rudy, Susan Wolfson, the staff at the Bodleian and English Faculty Libraries, Oxford and The Mistress and Fellows, Girton College, Cambridge. The British Academy Postdoctoral Fellowship, Corpus Christi, Oxford and the Victoria listserv have also provided invaluable support. This book is for my parents.

Biographical Outlines

FELICIA HEMANS

1793   Felicia Dorothea Browne born in Liverpool to George Browne, a merchant of aristocratic Irish descent and Felicity Dorothea (née) Wagner, daughter of the Consul at Liverpool for Austria and Tuscany; one of seven children.

1799   Father closes his Liverpool business amidst financial difficulties; the family move to Abergele, North Wales.

1800   First poems, including 'Lines on her Mother's Birthday'.

1808   *Poems*, dedicated to the Prince of Wales; read by Captain Alfred Hemans.

1809   *England and Spain, or Valour and Patriotism*. Family are evicted from their Abergele home; move to St Asaph, North Wales; she contracts scarlet fever.

1810   Father leaves for Quebec and never returns.

1812   *The Domestic Affections, and Other Poems*. She marries Captain Hemans, whereon they move to Daventry, Northamptonshire.

1813   Arthur Hemans born; the Hemans family move to Bronwylfa, North Wales, to live with Felicia's mother.

1815   Publishes poem on *Waverley* in the *Edinburgh Annual Register*. George Willoughby Hemans born.

1816   *The Restoration of the Works of Art to Italy: A Poem*. Claude Lewis Hemans born.

1817   *Modern Greece: A Poem*. Henry William Hemans born.

1818   *Translations from Camoens, and Other Poets, with Original Poetry*. 'Stanzas on the Death of the Princess

Charlotte' published in *Blackwood's*. Captain Hemans deserts his family, shortly after which Charles Lloyd Hemans is born.

1819   *Tales, and Historic Scenes, in Verse.*

1820   *The Sceptic: A Poem; Stanzas to the Memory of the Late King; Wallace's Invocation to Bruce.*

1821   Wins Royal Society of Literature prize for *Dartmoor: A Poem.*

1822   *Selection of Welsh Melodies, with Symphonies and Accompaniments by John Parry, and Characteristic Words By Mrs Hemans.*

1823   *The Siege of Valencia: A Dramatic Poem; The Last Constantine: with Other Poems; The Vespers of Palermo: A Tragedy in Five Acts.*

1824   *Lays of Many Lands. Vespers* staged in Edinburgh.

1825   *The Forest Sanctuary: and Other Poems.* Moves to Rhyllon with three youngest sons, mother and sister, Harriet.

1827   Mother dies.

1828   *Records of Woman, with other Poems.* Moves to Wavertree, Liverpool with sons; meets Henry Chorley, Mary Howitt and Maria Jane Jewsbury.

1830   *Songs of the Affections, with other Poems.* Stays with Wordsworth at Rydal Mount.

1833   *Hymns on the Works of Nature, for the Use of Children.*

1834   *Scenes and Hymns of Life, with other Religious Poems,* dedicated to Wordsworth. *National Lyrics, and Songs for Music.* Essay on Goethe's *Tasso* published in the *New Monthly Magazine.* Visits Wicklow, Ireland, for health reasons.

1835   Dies in Wicklow, most likely of rheumatic fever.

1836   *Poetical Remains of the Late Mrs Hemans.*

1839   *The Works of Mrs Hemans, with a Memoir of her Life by her Sister* published in seven volumes

1840   *Early Blossoms; a Collection of Poems Written Between Eight and Fifteen Years of Age, with a Life of the Authoress.*

DORA GREENWELL

1821   'Dorothy' Greenwell born at Greenwell Ford near Lanchester in Durham to William Thomas Greenwell, a squire and magistrate, and Dorothy (née) Smales, daughter of a Durham solicitor; one of five children.

1840   Receives medical treatment from Henry Jephson in Leamington Spa.

1842   Moves briefly to Italy for health reasons.

1848   First collection of poetry published as *Poems*. Father bankrupts the family.

1850   *Stories that Might be True, with other Poems*. Greenwells move to Ovingham in Northumberland where she meets Josephine Butler, feminist campaigner against the 1860s Contagious Diseases Acts. Move again to Golbourne Rectory in Lancashire, where her brother, Alan, is a High Church minister.

1854   Father dies; she and her now invalid mother relocate to Durham.

1855   *A Present Heaven: Letters to a Friend*.

1859   Begins writing to the famous publishing family, the Constables, her intellectual confidants and main source of cultural life; through them meets William Bell Scott.

1860   First visit to the Constables in Edinburgh.

1862   *Two Friends. The Patience of Hope*, dedicated to Josephine Butler. 'On Single Women' published in the *Northern British Review*.

1863   Begins corresponding with William Knight, Professor of Moral Philosophy at St Andrews, a minister of the Church of Scotland and eminent Victorian editor of the Wordsworths.

1865   Collaborates with Jean Ingelow and others on a book of poetry for children, *Home Thoughts and Home Scenes*.

1866   *Essays*.

1867   *Lacordaire*.

1868   'On the Education of the Imbecile' published in the *Northern British Review*. Suffers from a paralytic seizure from which she suffers the rest of her life.

1869   *Carmina Crucis*.

1870	Protests for the victims of the Irish Famine of 1847 and the Lancashire Cotton Famine of 1863.
1871	*Colloquia Crucis, A Sequel to 'Two Friends'; John Woolman.* Mother dies. Moves between London, Torquay and Clifton.
1873	*The Soul's Legend; Songs of Salvation.* 'The East African Slave Trade' published in the *Contemporary Review.*
1874	Moves to Westminster, London.
1875	*Liber Humanitatis: A Series of Essays on Various Aspects of Spiritual and Social Life.* Meets Christina Rossetti at All Saints Missions Home, Clifton.
1876	*Camera Obscura.*
1877	*A Basket of Summer Fruit.*
1881	Suffers an accident while living alone in Richmond, rendering her dependent on her brother Alan, with whom she moves in at Clifton.
1882	Dies of accident-related illness; buried in Arno's Vale Cemetery, Bristol.
1885	William Dorling's *Memoirs of Dora Greenwell* published.
1889	Dorling's *Poems, Selected, With a Biographical Introduction* published.

ADELAIDE ANNE PROCTER

1825	Adelaide Anne born in London to the poet, Bryan Waller Procter and Anne Benson (née) Skepper, renowned hostess of Victorian literary parties; one of six children.
1832	Family moves to St John's Wood, London.
1843	'Ministering Angels' published in *Heath's Book of Beauty.*
1848	William Makepeace Thackeray courts her.
1849	Thackeray quarrels with her and her mother.
1850	Attends Queen's College, Harley Street, where her tutors include F. D. Maurice, Charles Kingsley, John Hullah and Henry Morley. A guest at the reception George Smith throws to honour Charlotte Brontë's visit to London.

1851   Converts to Roman Catholicism (Bessie Parkes suggests she may have converted earlier, in 1849).

1853   Submits poems to Dickens's periodical, *Household Words*, using the pseudonym 'Mary Berwick'. Spends the year in Italy with her aunt Emily de Viry.

1854   'Words upon the Waters' and 'Hidden Light' published in *Household Words*. Dickens discovers the true identity of 'Miss Berwick'.

1856   'Watch Cry: from a German Patois Song' published in *Household Words*.

1858   *The Englishwoman's Journal* launched (runs until 1864). 'First Series' of *Legends and Lyrics*. Romantic involvement with Matilda M. Hays.

1859   'Letter reporting on a visit to a watch-making factory in Christchurch, Dorset' and 'Adventures of Your Own Correspondents in Search of Solitude' published in *The Englishwoman's Journal*. Society for Promoting the Employment of Women established.

1860   Part I of 'Madame Récamier' published in *The Englishwoman's Journal*. Emily Faithfull founds the Victoria Press. Hays's affair with Theodosia Monson and consequent rift with Procter.

1861   'Second Series' of *Legends and Lyrics* published. Parts II and III of 'Madame Récamier' published in *The Englishwoman's Journal*. Edits *The Victoria Regia: A Volume of Original Contributions in Poetry and Prose*. Attends the Portfolio Society, group of women artists and writers.

1862   *A Chaplet of Verses* published to raise money for the Providence Row Catholic Night Refuge for Homeless Women and Children in East London. Barbara Bodichon and Bessie Parkes ask Hays to leave *The English Woman's Journal* after her behaviour toward Procter.

1863   Becomes ill; takes cure at Malvern.

1864   Dies from excessive exhaustion; buried in Kensal Green Cemetery, London.

1866   Dickens's edition of her collected poetry published.

1877   'A Lost Chord' set to music by Sir Arthur Sullivan.

1881   *The Angel's Story*.

1

Introduction

A poet is somebody who feels, and who expresses his
feeling through words. This may sound easy. It isn't. A lot
of people think or believe or know they feel – but that's
thinking or believing or knowing; not feeling. And poetry
is feeling – not knowing or believing or thinking.[1]

All the earth's woes are there only to vanish before the
pure brilliance of a religious feeling.[2]

In her essay, 'On the Character of Mrs Hemans' Writings,'
Letitia Elizabeth Landon declared: 'There cannot be a greater
error than to suppose that the poet does not feel what he
writes. What an extraordinary, I might say, impossible view, is
this to take of an art more connected with emotion than any of
its sister sciences.'[3] Certainly Landon, like the subject of her
monologue, was celebrated in the early nineteenth century as
a poet of feeling. Women's capacity for extreme feeling was the
subject of much debate in this period, Mary Wollstonecraft
believing it a burden of gender where novelists such as Mary
Hays valued the individuality to be found in effusing the cries
of the human heart.[4] Yet the kind of feeling Felicia Hemans
both promoted and became associated with was quite different
from that attributed to Della Cruscans like Landon or dissenters like Wollstonecraft or Hays. Della Cruscanism's self-
conscious displays of emotion were regarded as provincial and
feigned against the apparently 'genuine' and profoundly
religious feelings Hemans sought to render, while rationally
rooted dissenters would have bristled at her poetic overflows
of emotion. Hemans, however, as well as Dora Greenwell and
Adelaide Anne Procter, struggled to find a mode of writing

1

able to communicate an emotive yet holy religious feeling, a struggle complicated further by their position as female poets, or 'poetesses'.

The questions the three women consequently raise in their poetry are difficult ones, and force the reader to address current critical attitudes, as well as contemporary ones, towards emotion, religion and politics. Their clear privileging of feeling in faith, social activism and lyric expression is not readily addressed within literary studies as it stands, a field preoccupied not with the intangible and religious, but with the material and secular.[5] Yet the sort of femininity these women claimed as inherent to their identity as people and poets was grounded in feeling, impulsive, irrational and gushing. While such an identity may seem over-determined to modern readers, adhering to male categories of the feminine, it was women's assumed receptivity to sensation that rendered them ideally suited to the vocation of poet. This apparent susceptibility to emotion was reinforced further in debates concerning sensibility, women deemed proficient at feeling refined emotion and then displaying it pastorally through compassion for the suffering of others. This was not Keatsian melancholy nor that 'luxury of grief' Leslie Stephen deemed sentimentalism.[6] Rather it had a religious and moral dimension which poets like the politically conservative Hannah More or the more radical thinker Anna Barbauld encouraged. For More, 'all actions, feelings, sentiments, tastes and passions' must be referred to 'the love and fear of God' in order to sustain a decorous and prudent nation state.[7] Barbauld agreed, but with more emphasis upon the power of emotion within religion, that which she eloquently declared 'an affair' of 'feeling', its seat 'in the imagination and the passions' and its 'source in that relish for the sublime, the vast, the beautiful'.[8] 'It is safer to trust to our genuine feelings, feelings implanted in us by the God of nature,' she declared, 'than to any metaphysical subtleties', a distinction one makes through the 'charms of poetry'.[9]

If women were considered the moral and religious guardians of a rapidly changing society, the female poet had even more power, poetry being considered the holiest of genres throughout the period, as critics from John Dennis to John Keble suggested. Yet poetry, like religion, was beginning to seem outdated and irrelevant, the novel dominating the literary market of the later nineteenth century. Hemans literally came to the rescue for some, as one critic claimed in the *Edinburgh Monthly Review*. 'Every one knows', he wrote, 'the recent remarkable history of poetry, and its present actual predicament'. The 'high temperature of Lord Byron's poetry, for a time, kept from cooling the mass of public feeling', but now, it seems, there is a danger that the same readers are 'off to novels'. He invites these deserters of poetry, however, to turn to Hemans as one of 'the first poets of the age' able to secure a 'permanent hold of our sympathies' by exciting 'emotion which endures, and which gives fresh delight on repetition, by expressing natural feeling, in a sweet flow of tenderness, or a sustained and deep tone of pathos'.[10] Just when poetry seemed to be in a decline, Hemans's volumes of verse became best-sellers, succeeded only by Procter, who sold more poetry than any of her contemporaries bar Tennyson. The less popular but equally respected Greenwell too may be viewed as practically obsessed with the role of poet and how she might fulfil it as both a Christian and political liberal. As Isobel Armstrong reminds us, our group of three are also united in their focus on 'political matters', invested in producing a humane lyricism that would respect everyone equally as thinking and feeling organisms.[11]

Many women poets, however, including the three discussed here, did not oppose the political to the personal, instead regarding social action as being motivated by the subject's ability to feel. The connection between feeling, virtue and social responsibility may be traced back to the eighteenth century, but for Hemans, Greenwell and Procter, the source of their interest in feeling was Wordsworth.[12] Hemans was profoundly influenced by the laureate, her later poetry in particular mirroring his spiritual and nature-based concerns; Greenwell's intellectual confidant, William Knight, was the most prominent and respected of Wordsworth's Victorian editors; and Procter, the daughter of Wordsworth's friend 'Barry Cornwall', was also moved by Keble's *Lectures on Poetry* (1832–41), dedicated to Wordsworth. Moreover, the kind of expressive theory that marked much nineteenth-century poetics was, as Armstrong suggests, rooted in Wordsworth's overflow of feeling notion, one delineated in his Preface to the *Lyrical Ballads* (1802). Here, Wordsworth claimed that poetry as a form would only be sustained if poets wrote in such a way that the common reader would understand – a 'language really used by men' but one granted 'a certain colouring of imagination' that would appeal to the heart. 'For all good poetry', he declared, 'is the spontaneous overflow of powerful feelings', feelings 'modified and directed by our thoughts, which are indeed the representatives of all our past feelings'.[13] Feelings, then, give rise to thoughts which reflect former emotions, and everything the poet sees, experiences or touches is filtered through his empathetic reaction to it: poetry becomes not a photographic record but one of personal response.[14] As G. Kim Blank suggests, Wordsworth's philosophy forwards the idea that the self is established by the ability to feel, a fundamentally democratic impulse to which everyone has access.[15] Even those who choose not to write can nevertheless approach the world in a poetic manner through emotion and gentle sensibility, according to Wordsworth, who, in 'When, to the attractions of the busy world' (1805), called his seafaring brother John a 'silent poet'. For while John 'convers[es] not', the narrator intimates, his tender character still enables him to develop from 'common feelings' and 'solitude' a 'watchful heart', 'an inevitable ear;/ And an eye practised like a blind man's touch'.[16] This affectionate and notably feminized way of forging identity and writing poetry helped to validate the female poet and certainly Hemans extended the laureate's attempt to bring thought to feeling and feeling to thought by merging the two as inseparable.

Hemans, Greenwell and Procter each encouraged their readers to think and feel at the same time when approaching their poetry, not least because of their religious convictions. For religious duty was founded on the profession of a reasoned knowledge of God as well as an experiential relationship with him. It was the feeling of such experience that remained paramount, and not issues of belief: while the women considered which denominational affiliation might suit them best, they were all firm believers. The transition their poetry does mark, then, is precisely one regarding the status of religious feeling in the period: we shall see how the emotional climate

4

so receptive to Hemans's work becomes marred by restraint and reserve by the time Procter is writing, 'gushiness' losing its sense of divinity and becoming quixotic or mawkish. Feeling, of course, remains pivotal throughout the nineteenth century, Tennyson's mournful poetics, Dickens's sentimentalism, the erratic ejaculations of the spasmodics and a gothicized sensation fiction all popular with Victorian readers. Yet the kind of explicitly christian feeling Hemans promotes gradually vanishes from the sphere of literary taste, and what remains of it is a mere residue of the kind of feelings outlined above, increasingly associated with the almost hysterical, rather than refined, strains of evangelical writing. For Greenwell, the very suitability of an emotive poetics to the forwarding of God's word becomes questionable, her prose inquiry into the compatibility of poetics and christianity an insight into her own sometimes clumsy verse.[17] For Greenwell, the problem is precisely one of feeling, poetry exciting too much within the individual, distracting him or her from God and demanding 'food for a "darker ecstasy" ' than that christianity seeks.[18] Procter's reaction is to engage in strong feeling by compressing it into the tiny frames of hymnal stanzas, holding back emotion but in the process demonstrating its centrality to her faith. The rest of this introduction will discuss these issues in more detail by addressing, first, the women's roles as 'poetesses'; second, their shared tendency to favour the lyric form over other genres of poetry; and finally, the importance they granted religion in their literary and spiritual careers.

'POETESSES'

The women discussed here are referred to as 'nineteenth-century' poets in order to free them from periodic constraint, little of their work according wholly to traditional notions of 'Romantic' or 'Victorian'. For Hemans and Procter, and at times Greenwell too, the category of 'poetess' or 'female poet' branded their reputations, rendering both their work and their very being feminine and emotive. Such branding was usually enforced by male critics, Alexander Dyce's *Specimens of British Poetesses* (1825), Frederick Rowton's *The Female Poets of Great*

Britain (1848) and Eric S. Robertson's *English Poetesses* (1883), each full of praise and admiration for those anthologized within but deeming them worthy by internally constructing the women as moral pinnacles.[19] As H. N. Coleridge stated in 'Modern English Poetesses' (1840): 'When we venture to lift a pen against women, straightway *apparent facies*; the weapon drops pointless on the marked passage; and whilst the mind is bent on praise or censure of the poem, the eye swims too deep in tears and mist over the poetess herself in the frontispiece, to let it see its way to either'.[20] Representing selfless, charitable, domestic virtue, often in the guise of suffering womanhood, the poetess intensifies the melancholy role once occupied by male poets, more ardent and more passionate than the tradition from which she emerges. Compare the above commentary, for example, to John Gibson Lockhart's infamous response to feeling male poets in his *Blackwood's* article, 'On the Cockney School of Poetry' (1817–19), wherein Hunt, Keats and Hazlitt, as well as Procter's father, were condemned for their mellifluous, sensual and deeply felt poetry.[21] Such weaknesses were deemed the strength of the poetess, who, by the prescription of her sex, was the embodiment of such metaphysical 'feminine qualities', affect, beauty, spirituality, that when Samuel Taylor Coleridge envisioned the ideal thinker it was a figure with a male mind and female soul.[22]

Yet for Coleridge this ideal described the androgynous man and was not open to actual women, who had to deal with the constrictions of their gender. In the Preface to his edition of Hemans's poems, for example, William Michael Rossetti argued: 'One might sum up the weak points in Mrs Hemans' poetry by saying that it is not only "feminine" poetry' but 'also "female" poetry: besides exhibiting the fineness and charm of womanhood, it has the monotone of mere sex'.[23] Directed by the 'guiding power of morals or religion', Hemans produces a poetry which has 'the emotional gush of a spontaneous sentiment', a description that summarizes Wordsworth's poetic, but presupposes a certain lack of control in women that the manly laureate rose above. Like many critics, William Godwin considered women to 'have a frame of body more delicate and susceptible of impression than men, and, in proportion as they receive a less intellectual education, are more unreservedly under the empire of feeling'.[24] While his lover, Wollstonecraft, was considered to possess a philosophical strength of reasoned feeling, poetesses were not. The Countess of Blessington iterated the poetess's dreamy yet whimsical status further when she mused in her parodic 'Stock in Trade of Modern Poetesses' (1833), 'Bursting tear and endless sigh –/ *Query* – can she tell us why?'[25] No wonder Hemans grumbled of her deriders: 'If I were in higher spirits, I should be strongly tempted to do something *very* strange amongst them, in order to fulfil the ideas I imagine they entertain of that altogether foreign monster, a *Poetess*, but I feel too much subdued for such *capricci* at present'.[26]

The poetess profession nevertheless remained one of considerable commercial power at least through the 1830s and 1840s, during which the gift-book and annual craze was at its height. For all those who regarded the role as merely sentimental, many understood it as part of a mythical cult of genius beginning with Sappho, and heralded in our period by the female laureate heroine of Madame de Staël's *Corinne, or Italy* (1807). Mary Robinson was insistent on Sappho's inspirational role as a 'Grecian Muse' in her introductory notes to *Sappho and Phaon* (1796) and the adventurous Landon took to publicly dressing as the improvisatrice in a flamboyantly Sapphic costume.[27] Corinne herself owns Sapphic qualities, initially crowned as a Petrarchan poetess, instituted as the voice of the Italian nation, but finally suffering a tragic demise. The novel had a profound effect upon many women writers and Hemans declared that it 'has a power over me which is quite indescribable; some passages seem to give me back my own thoughts and feelings, my whole inner being with a mirror, more true than ever friend could hold up'. Hemans's French edition of *Corinne* is covered with her protesting identifications with the heroine, and Chorley tells us that the words 'C'est moi' are marked against one of the laureate's many descriptions regarding the close proximity of poetry to feeling.[28] As Corinne asserts, 'poetry captivates the senses as well as the mind', and, for her at least, forwards a kind of peculiarly Italian 'sparkling melody' that lies in contrast to the melancholic tones of English verse.[29] The mythic figure of Corinne, then, at once deeply emotional and politically vocal, remained an appealing model for women poetesses. Foreign, female and feminized, she was entirely removed both from the didactic poetical style by which Wordsworth was so repelled, and from the rationalist mode made chic within the works of the bluestockings.

The poetess's natural genius, immense capacity for feeling and youthful allure contributed, however, to an image of a woman lacking formal education and the kind of philosophic depth the overflowing Wordsworth was granted. Intellectual women responded to the role cautiously, Elizabeth Barrett Browning eager to remind her readers that: 'Poetry has been as serious a thing to me as life itself [. . .] I never mistook pleasure for the final cause of poetry; nor leisure, for the hour of the poet'.[30] If the relationship between poetry, thought and feeling preoccupied those writing within the nineteenth century, it continues to be debated by critics today. For Daniel Karlin, the shift from fancy to fervour in women's poetry meant that many women became far too earnest, negating the splendours of the pleasure principle Wordsworth's Preface acclaimed.[31] Anne K. Mellor even separates the affective poetess from what she calls the 'female poet', the latter an 'explicitly political' identity situated within the public sphere.[32] She argues that by focusing on sentimentalism, critics ignore those women who rooted their poetry in the radical writings of seventeenth-century female preachers and prophets. These women, spurred by Quakers, Methodists and the Dissenting Academies, invoked scriptural authority for the right to speak in public, and in turn, inaugurated a tradition of feminist, political and didactic women's poetry. Yet for Virginia Blain, both Karlin and Mellor are misguided, the former overlooking the problems women may have experienced in attempting to write purely from a motive of pleasure, and the latter imposing an overly 'rigid divide' between feeling and thinking poetry.[33] Armstrong too clarifies Mellor's argument by suggesting that while many women poets refused to consent to the idea of a distinct feminine, non-rational and effusive discourse, those who did often exploited affective language to think with.[34] Before turning to the nature of such thought, which is strikingly religious, we must consider that generic form best suited to thinking through feeling; that is, the lyric.

LYRIC

The lyric readily evokes feeling because of its non-narrative and non-dramatic form, recognizable by its musical quality and song-like metres. The lyric's roots in the word lyre attests to this musicality, but also emphasize the pain associated with this very personal and subjective form. When Hermes, god of communication, invented the lyre, he took its components from various animal parts, so producing music from the suffering of living beings. This tradition, as Catherine Maxwell argues, has marked the development of the lyric, a genre continually associated with anguish and loss and so an ideal medium through which marginalized groups like women might voice their concerns.[35] It is as if the beauty and intensity the lyric achieves compensates those who are powerless in society, as the Ovidian tale of Philomela recalls: raped by an aggressor who cuts out her tongue, Philomela, whose name means 'lover of song', is magically turned into a nightingale to escape further violence. By the Romantic era, the nightingale, singing its melancholy and impassioned song, became synonymous with the lyric poet, and Shelley declared in 1821: 'A poet is a nightingale, who sits in darkness and sings to cheer its own solitude with sweet sounds; his auditors are as men entranced by the melody of an unseen musician, who feel that they are moved and softened, yet know not whence or why'.[36] This feminized poetics of privacy was reconceived by John Stuart Mill as 'feeling confessing itself to itself, in moments of solitude', poetry understood as the only genre suited to conveying the poet's inner processes, mental and emotional, in linguistic terms.[37] It is not surprising, perhaps, that Wordsworth's favourite of Hemans's poems was 'For a Picture of St Cecilia Attended By Angels', notably because of the address to the nightingale forwarded in the fifth verse.[38]

Subjective and personal, then, the lyric imaginatively renders emotional states, verbalizing feelings that otherwise might not be conveyed in linear or descriptive terms, such as religious or mystical experience, or love. While the feelings conveyed are private, they are still offered to an audience who, as Shelley claimed, would be 'softened', or as Hemans would put it, christianized. Wordsworth reshaped the lyric into a

9

balladic form, endowing it with a popular or folk element that was traditionally conveyed orally within a community. It is this kind of communitarian lyric that Hemans adopts, standing amidst her audience to transmit a religious message she believed would unite her listeners within a common bond of emotional and spiritual feeling. The lyric offered the best route to the democratic dissemination of spirituality not only because of its ability to represent feeling but also due to its inherent opposition, and therefore resistance, to the increasingly material and reified world of the nineteenth century.[39] Deriving its authority from feeling, rather than from education or knowledge, the lyric was open to everyone, and became a useful way of critiquing society, especially for those who felt excluded from the usual ways of effecting change.[40] Feelings, then, were granted a sort of special power within the lyric form and Hemans grasped it as a way of encouraging her readers to feel more deeply about the world around them. Hemans even feared that the current state of the lyric underestimated the degree of feeling needed to carry religious messages, and related in the Preface to *Scenes and Hymns of Life* (1834) how she had endeavoured 'to enlarge' the 'sphere of Religious Poetry, by associating with its themes more of the emotions' than some poets had previously admitted.[41] The lyric not only enabled her to express emotion but suggested to her readers that they should reciprocate, like Wordsworth's silent poet, with a suitably emotional response. Doing so, Hemans thought, would gently push them towards religion, the prime location of feeling and love and the only force available that mirrored poetry's ability to provide 'healing relief' from the vagaries and cruelties of life.[42]

Greenwell, however, was not so sure. All three poets discussed here recognized the lyric as an affirming force of religion, and yet Greenwell worried that it would come to distract the subject from God altogether. Her poetry, theological essays and social commentaries all work to try and reconcile the interests of art and religion but sometimes struggle to do so, Greenwell fearing that aesthetics would consume the subject and leave no space for the contemplation of God. The debate she sets forth in her prose is founded upon countless epigraphs taken from both religious and literary figures through whom she voices her swinging opinions regarding the role and expression of faith in society. Like Hemans, Greenwell considered the decline of poetry to be connected to the deterioration of both christian and moral values, recognizing that powerful feeling was needed to quicken an emotionally blunted nation. Yet at the same time she fears the pouring forth of feeling as that which might drown her faith even as she is unable to control her expression. This produces a poetry which seems literally to ache for direction, begging its reader to decide on the tone but equally allowing a freedom of interpretation that grants the religious quality within a meaning for readers of all faiths or none. Procter, however, retreats almost altogether from both Hemans's explicit defence of religious feeling and Greenwell's apprehensive stance by holding back the expression of intense emotion within her lyric verse. This is perhaps a kind of anxiety of influence on her behalf, Hemans's popularity still immense by the time the young Procter begins to write, and her father's impassioned poetry well known, if controversial.[43] Yet Procter's inability to gush forth poetically is not only related to her fear of the criticism her father had received for articulating deep feeling in his poetry. For her poetic reticence was related both to her early Tractarian faith, which demanded the holding back of strong religious feeling; and also to her romantic leanings, which, when permitted, had proved greatly painful. She seems to have broken at least one engagement and endured the most intense of affairs with the capricious Matilda Hays, by whom she was at first enchanted and finally destroyed.

In declaring her love for God, then, Procter remained cautious, not from a lack of faith but from a suspicion of effusively exhibiting feeling. Her 'reserve', a word that for Tractarians signified the withdrawal of religious belief within to protect it from the onslaughts of worldliness, may have been one of the central reasons for her investment in poetry, the most oblique and guarded of genres.[44] As Keble argued in his *Lectures*, 'that Almighty Power, which governs and har- monises, not heaven and earth only, but also the hearts of men, has furnished amplest comfort for sufferers of either kind in the gift of Poetry'.[45] Filtered through a religious mind, poetry

11

becomes 'a kind of medicine divinely bestowed upon man: which gives healing relief to secret mental emotion'; like the lover who 'needs but very few notes to convey his real meaning to sympathetic hearts', those who experience genuine religious feeling do not need to shout it loudly.[46] Indeed the test of the authentic religious poet for Keble is one that proves able to 'lightly touch' on theological ideas in verse as a marker of their truth, refraining from spilling out that which is precious to the believer but prone to misinterpretation or even ridicule by secular readers.[47] Concealed behind a poetical shield, however, religious notions and feelings become a kind of code which readers must work to decipher by drawing on their own belief systems, whatever they may be. This, Keble thought, was why Wordsworth had held such popular appeal, his poetry containing such a force of authentic feeling that, 'whether he sang of Man or of Nature Failed not to Lift up Men's Hearts to Holy Things'.[48] Rather than backing any specific set of doctrines, however, Wordsworth's poetry tended to celebrate belief itself, rendering the world a religious stage on which we form relationships guided by religious feeling.[49]

RELIGION

Like Wordsworth, all three women addressed here sought to lift up their readers to 'holy things', going beyond the soft and nebulous benevolence of the eighteenth century to celebrate a more energetic and distinctively christian kind of feeling. The dynamism of religion in their lives has tended to be under-estimated by modern secular critics who often condemn poets like Hemans, Greenwell and Procter for the very reasons their work was published and read by a large, popular readership.[50] The presence of women poets in religious anthologies and hymnals of the age is striking and the explicitly christian messages they attempted to advocate within such contributions were regarded as genuinely felt by readers.[51] For it is her capacity for religious feeling that rendered the woman poet the ideal advocate of moral, and specifically religious values, as George Gilfillan remarks in his essay 'Mrs Hemans'. 'Females', he writes, 'may be called the natural guardians of morality and faith. These shall always be safe in the depths of the female intellect, and of the female heart – an intellect, the essence of which is worship – a heart, the element of which is love.'[52] Gilfillan's assertion returns us to the balance of feeling and thought women poets both considered they could achieve and were expected to effect, not only factually apprehending God but conveying his reality through the ethereal strains of verse. Moreover, if poetry was the genre closest to God because of its mysterious and reticent nature, an argument John Henry Newman promoted along with Keble, then the poet was instantly granted an almost spiritual status.[53] As Thomas Carlyle maintained in 'The Hero as Poet' (1841): 'Prophet and Poet, well understood, have much kindred of meaning. Fundamentally indeed they are still the same; in this most important respect especially, that they have penetrated both of them into the sacred mystery of the Universe.'[54]

While poetry as a form has been linked to religious utterance since the early modern period, by the nineteenth century, as Cynthia Scheinberg argues, it had become the key site for presenting and exploring distinctions between religious perspectives.[55] The explosion of varying belief systems within Protestantism alone is overwhelming, the Religious Census in 1851 recording thirty separate nonconformist traditions. The period was also marked by a Roman Catholic renaissance; the emergence of the Oxford Movement and Anglo-Catholicism; the rapid expansion of Judaism; and a new awareness of holistic and spiritual philosophy such as Tao, Vedanta, Buddhism and Sufism.[56] Within this profound religious diversity, poetry was elevated as the defender of all faiths, Matthew Arnold declaring in his essay 'The Study of Poetry' (1880) that the 'strongest part of our religion to-day is its unconscious poetry'.[57] Hemans, Greenwell and Procter strived to uphold quite different ideas of faith as poets, but importantly refused to align themselves with one set of denominational doctrines within christianity, all three, to a greater or lesser extent, blurring the boundaries between religious groups. Greenwell is the most extraordinary of the three women in this respect, a theologian and a pious christian but commenting widely on religions as disparate as Evangelicalism, Roman Catholicism and Islam. She seems to have practised a kind of bricolaged christianity which confounded onlookers, her close friend Elizabeth McChesney describing Greenwell's faith as 'very bewildering' and one which evinced a love for 'the Quakers' which became more pronounced still for 'the Methodists', even though 'she loved all the main doctrines of Rome' and considered herself 'High Church'.[58] Procter too was initially captivated by Tractarianism before converting to Roman Catholicism in 1851, a move out of which emerged the deeply ceremonial *A Chaplet of Verses* (1862). So stirring was this collection that, on reading it, Procter's Quaker friend Bessie Parkes was also persuaded to Rome, but in both cases, conversion has none of the trauma and angst associated with Newman's equivalent change of heart. While doctrinal specificities were important to the women addressed here, and certainly Greenwell has the theologian's capacity to distinguish them, they ultimately held little charm when compared with the more significant experiential space prayer and faith created.

The emotional intensity that drives much of Hemans's poetry, for example, is recognizably Anglican, but also possesses a spiritual strength that goes beyond the dictates of denomination. This is not to say that her work is not christian, volumes such as her sonnet sequence *Female Characters of Scripture* (1834), a testament to her faithful love of the Bible. But rather than advocating certain beliefs, Hemans strived to 'follow the direction of a lofty spiritual melancholy', as Schiller described it, by composing poems she believed would propel the reader into a state of intense religious feeling. Hemans referred to this feeling as affection, a word that signified the fusion of feeling and thought in one's relationship to God as pointed out by many eighteenth-century theologians such as Isaac Watts and John Wesley.[59] Schiller forwarded the same kind of idea in terms of poetry, writing in his famous essay 'On Simple and Sentimental Poetry' (1795) that the best poets were those who combined ideas with emotions in addressing spiritual, rather than didactic, themes.[60] This 'convulser of the heart', as Coleridge called him, held immeasurable appeal to both Hemans and Greenwell because of this theory, Schiller being a philosopher who, as Michael John Kooy suggests, espoused a kind of aesthetic humanism designed to move readers by raising standards of taste.[61] Such humanism should be spiritually rooted but doctrinally liberal, Schiller suggested, one of the fragments in his series of short dialogues 'Votive Tablets' reading: 'Which religion do I acknowledge? None that thou namest. "None that I name? And why so?" – Why, for religion's own sake!'[62] This quip reflects the philosopher's own personal trajectory with regard to religion: he reluctantly chose a medical career when his college refused to train him as a Protestant pastor, but found within science an emphasis upon corporeal feeling that would affect his views on spirituality.[63] Religion came to signify a benign channelling of feelings for Schiller, that without such direction had the potential to lapse into a revelling in the senses. He considered feelings, however, to own a supernatural force that could be captured within the lyric, single sentiments expressed in a few words with tremendous power to provoke the reader into philosophical consideration. Hemans certainly preferred Schiller's lyric poetry, asking a friend to send her 'not the plays, but the poems' when staying with Wordsworth in 1830. 'Mr Wordsworth', Hemans wrote, 'wants to read a little of Schiller with me, and he is not to be had at Ambleside [. . .] Indeed, I think he is inclined to undervalue German literature from not knowing its best and purest masterpieces.' 'I', she asserts, 'shall try to bring him into a better way of thinking, if only out of my own deep love for what has been to me a source of intellectual joy so cheering and elevating.'[64]

The solace Hemans found in late eighteenth-century German literature issued in part from its reaction against Sturm and Drang, consisting as it did of a move away from the destructive emotion associated with this movement to a newly spiritualized mode of utterance.[65] Like Schiller, Hemans sought a way of communicating God's word through an emotional lyric expressivity that departed, on one hand, from the didactic literature that had preceded her and, on the other, from the extremes of religious feeling to be found in enthusiasm. The dangers and fervour of enthusiastic feeling had been furiously debated in the eighteenth century, and arguably it is what formed the foundation for Romantic notions of the imagination.[66] As Jon Mee argues, a characteristic feature of Romanticism was its desire to grasp the authenticity of emotional expression which that enthusiasm signified while at the same time distancing itself from the more vulgar and impulsive aspects of enthusiasm.[67] Later, such feeling would ground Victorian conceptions of the tender 'heart' as the nerve centre of christianity, scientizing emotion and rendering its excessive expression an illness Freud's psychoanalytic project came to address.[68] Indeed, unlike the more refined feelings associated with sensibility or affection, enthusiastic feeling could affect or infect anyone, a divinely inspired emotion that sent believers off into rapturous and demented states from which they sometimes did not return. Many conservative critics condemned enthusiasm as vulgar and riotous, a form of feeling to which women were regarded especially prey, threatening as it did to destroy their virtue and feminine integrity. The care Hemans, Procter and Greenwell take to convey religious feeling is in part a reaction against enthusiasm, the three poets endeavouring to find a manner of lyric expressivity able to convey their love of God without falling into extremes of emotion. In this sense, the reader cannot simply push these women into a tradition of female mysticism or prophecy: their work is a far cry from the inspirited declarations of Joanna Southcott, for example. Yet neither are they defensive about feeling as Ann Radcliffe was, her Burkean accounts of emotional women suppressing feeling contrary to the project Hemans, Greenwell and Procter initiate.[69] Feeling remains a force they alternately guard against, believe to be the root of benevolence and consider as the basis of the modern self, but it is above all religious for the women and it is this emphasis the following study will explore.

2

Felicia Hemans

'I speak from feeling alone', wrote Felicia Hemans in 1828, a telling comment from the pen of the most widely read woman poet of the nineteenth century.[1] 'Feeling' in Hemans's poetry is crucial, as reviews of her work from the Romantic, Victorian and modern eras attest, each focusing on her use of emotion and sensibility, whether to praise or disparage it. When, in 1891, Mackenzie Bell proposed the writing of an essay on the 'rise and fall of the sentimental in English poetry', he thought that Hemans should be at its crown, echoing Frederic Rowton's focus on her 'delicacy,' 'softness,' 'pureness,' 'quick observant vision,' and 'ready sensibility'.[2] Eric Robertson agreed that her expression of 'subjective feeling' was pivotal; William Michael Rossetti proclaimed her style one that owned 'a readiness approaching improvisation'; and Arthur Symons championed Hemans's capacity to write from 'genuine feeling and with easy spontaneity'.[3] Even Gary Kelly, Hemans's most recent editor, affirms that her 'strategy is to write the heart'.[4] Feeling also helps us to reconcile the fact of her extreme popularity in the Romantic era with her dwindling status after the onset of modernism. As Symons declares: 'If poetry were really what the average person thinks it to be, an idealisation of the feelings, at those moments when the mind is open to every passing impression, ready to catch at similitudes and call up associations, but not in the grip of a strong thought or vital passion, then the verse of Felicia Hemans would be, as people once thought it was, the ideal poetry'.[5] She excelled, he intimates, because of her use of a particular kind of feeling that infringed upon neither the passions nor the intellect. 'The poetry of Mrs Hemans', Robertson wrote, 'lacks any note of supreme passion', while Rowton insisted that 'to *passion* she is well nigh a stranger'.[6] In her modernist assessment of the 1830s, Janet E. Courtney even declared, 'we do not go to Mrs Hemans' for 'profundity of thought', but 'for sensitive femininity, for perception of natural beauty, for heroic sentiment, for graceful and tender tributes to "the domestic affections" '.[7]

Yet late eighteenth- and early nineteenth-century readers *did* go to Hemans for profundity of thought and the expression of feeling, partly because of her ability to fuse the two in her poetry, and also to manoeuvre around the extremities of passion.[8] Hemans privileged 'affection' as a special kind of feeling that did not differentiate between reason and emotion. The word affection itself was rooted in eighteenth-century theological and philosophical treatises on the way the human body and mind work together. We will return to these treatises later, but for now it is important to note how Hemans's lyrical expression of affection and overflowing feeling did not signify the same thing for eighteenth- and nineteenth-century readers as it does for us. This is because literary taste shifted in the nineteenth century, and, as Marlon B. Ross suggests, Hemans's poetry marks what was clearly a crisis in taste at this time produced by the struggles and overlaps between 'masculine and feminine conduct, individualistic and collectivist social practice, genteel and bourgeois social status, elite and popular culture, Tory and Whig politics, and traditional and disruptive artistic forms'.[9] As Hemans's biographer, Charles William Sutton, declared, 'her poetry lacks deep thought or subtle emotion, and although it had immense popularity in its day, its sweetness and fluency have long palled upon the taste of thoughtful readers'.[10] Taste, as the French sociologist Pierre Bourdieu shows, is necessarily tied to any given culture's political investment in certain representations of such things as gender, class and race.[11] Accordingly, the 'Romantic' Hemans, the religious lyrist of the affections, differed from the 'Victorian' Hemans, who, as Tricia Lootens shows us, became an Enlightenment figure of domestic patriotism. In her Victorian incarnation, Hemans was seen as envisioning 'the glory of nationalism as international' and energizing the imperialist cause in a poetry that would prefigure the hardy strains of Rupert Brooke.[12] In the following period Hemans ceased to matter at all, partly because, as Ross argues, she could not exist in the modernist vision of what literature looked like, a picture in which feeling was irrevocably severed from thought.[13] As Ross argues: 'In Hemans' work there is no crisis of sensibility' and 'no irreparable break between thought and emotion', feeling being neither 'sentimental' nor indulgent, but rather the backbone of the intellect. Hemans's insistence on speaking from feeling alone, then, generates many questions about her role as a poet and how readers variously perceived her works on the home, nation, femininity and religion. This chapter will deal with each of these themes in turn, and suggest that Hemans's poetic project becomes more markedly religious as it evolves into a manifesto of religious feeling.

HOME AND HEARTH

In 1828 Hemans declared that, 'I have been all my life a creature of hearth and home', and her biographer, Henry Chorley, stresses the sense of refuge she found by the fireside.[14] For many readers she remains a guardian of the home and of family values, and yet this image, popularized by the Victorians, would have been less straightforward to Hemans. For the home, while certainly an idealized retreat in her poetry, was beloved as a sacred place where the material world and spiritual matters alike could be quietly contemplated. To understand why Hemans's readers would have acknowledged her representation of the home as a religious space, we must go back to her beginnings and the home in which she grew up. Hemans was born in Liverpool on 25 September 1793, daughter of the merchant and one-time Imperial and Tuscan consul, George Browne, and the half-German, half-Italian Felicity (née) Wagner, who introduced her to European languages, poetry, music and art. She was the fifth of seven, two brothers becoming soldiers in the Peninsular War, one brother a deputy assistant commissary-general in Canada and the remaining girls equally invested in literary pursuits. When her father's business suffered what Hemans's sister, Harriet Hughes, called 'commercial reverses', the family moved to Gwrych, near Abegele in North Wales, close to the sea and 'shut in by a picturesque range of mountains'.[15] Educated by her mother, Hemans was a quick student, introduced to mythological and classical allusions in art on a visit to the London galleries aged 11, and continuing through her life to read avidly and memorize poetry with considerable speed. Perhaps most impressive, however, was Hemans's grasp of languages: she learned French, Portuguese, Spanish and Italian from her mother, Latin from the local vicar, and devoted her life to what she thought the most 'rich and affectionate' language, German.[16] 'I never felt a more ardent emulation in the pursuit of excellence than at present,' she wrote in a letter to her aunt in 1808, 'knowledge, virtue and religion are the exalted objects of my enthusiastic wishes and fervent prayers.'[17]

Regarding herself as a scholar, then, and one with a particular investment in religion and fervent feeling, Hemans published her first quarto volume, *Poems*, in 1808. This included occasional and abstract pieces on subjects such as the family, genius and hope, some religious poems, and several sonnets written in the sentimental mode popularized by Charlotte Smith. The volume also comprised a number of patriotic and political poems that look forward to the publication of *England and Spain; or Valour and Patriotism* in the same year. The latter was filled with indirect admiration for her two elder brothers who were in Spain fighting against Napoleon, and their army friend, Captain Alfred Hemans, who quickly became a romantic admirer of their sister. While Mrs Browne protectively cut off Hemans's other possible suitor and literary fan, the notorious young Shelley, Alfred treated her daughter little better than the famous atheist had behaved toward Harriet Westbrook, and abandoned her in 1818 to live permanently in Rome. Having married Alfred in 1812, living with him in Daventry and Wales and bearing him five boys, Hemans betrayed nothing of her feelings towards him in print bar the figuration of romantic tragedy in her writing.[18] As Courtney suggests, the removal of her husband probably enhanced her literary career because it justified visits to Italy and intensified Hemans's studies of languages, classical art and poetics.[19] Arguably, it was her writing and increasing fame that alienated a husband who had met Hemans when she was only 15, a then fanciful girl infatuated with a captain of the

King's Own Regiment, rather than the mature poet she was to become.

The separation was a public one, and yet it did not detract from Hemans's growing popularity as a poet of home and hearth. As Kelly notes with reference to Hemans's successfully sustained 'femininity', to which we will return, Romantic poetics were upheld by the 'validation of discourse by the known character of the writer'.[20] In other words, the reading public was, as it remains, quick to judge writers whose lifestyle or perceived values departed from those presented in their work. So how did Hemans maintain her assured domestic voice amidst the scandal of her own affairs? This query provides the modern reader with a clue to the Romantics' notion of home, one marked as much by a sense of religious retreat as by marital convention. Hemans certainly evinced a christian sensibility, and L. B. Walford notes that it was her religious beliefs that prevented her from ever officially separating from Alfred Hemans.[21] To delve deeper into Hemans's configuration of the home, we might also turn to John Hollander's discussion of the poetical representation of the idea of 'home' as a foundation for the religiously inclined self. From the Renaissance interest in pilgrimage and 'homeward journeys', to Wordsworth's regard for a sacred domestic space, and the Victorians' obsession with the piety of the household, the home remains an anchor point for the individual of faith.[22] For the Romantics, the implication of home was that it provided a place to journey out from and return to, and so mirrored heaven as the source from which the soul issues forth at birth and to which it is restored in death. It was thus rendered a powerfully inviting domain combining strong religious feeling and nobility of thought, and so provoking the affections: as Hemans said of Wordsworth: 'This author is the true *Poet of Home*, and of all the lofty feelings which have their root in the soil of home affections'.[23] Nostalgia becomes the driving force that pushes one back home, and also that which highlights how rarely home is an actual fixed place, indicating rather an imagined mooring to which we are always tied, and also a sense of belonging. For Hemans, as for many of her readers, this anchor was God as well as the family – the latter, as she had found, an often unsatisfying, and unreliable, inevitability from which the only escape was the life of the mind, the spiritual and the supernatural.

When Hemans writes about the 'domestic affections', then, she is invoking a sense of home that is grounded in the emotions and mind, the imagination and christian faith. This is what so enthralled readers, as Rowton argued, who recognized the power, and not the forced security, of Hemans's portrayal of the home:

> In nothing can one trace her feminine spirit more strikingly than in her domestic *home*-loving ideas. Her first volume, written before she was fifteen, is chiefly about home: it is entitled *The Domestic Affections*; and is full of calm sweet pictures of most gentle and refining tendency [. . .] No where, indeed, can we find a more pure and refined idea of home than that which pervades Mrs Hemans' writings on the subject.[24]

The Domestic Affections and Other Poems (1812) was not, in fact, Hemans's first published work, but Rowton's commentary serves to remind us of the value placed on this early collection of her poetry during the nineteenth century. Affirming once more her 'feminine' qualities, Rowton underlines Hemans's success as a poet of those domestic affections for which she had praised Wordsworth. The domestic and the homely are, however, far from being sentimental codes for female household labour or modest family cosiness. The crowning poem of the volume, 'The Domestic Affections', reads as a succinct manifesto of Hemans's self-confessed priorities: knowledge, virtue and religion rather than needlework or cookery. As Wordsworth despaired during Hemans's visit to Rydal Mount, her 'education had been unfortunate' so as to leave her 'totally ignorant of housewifery' and 'as easily' able to manage 'the spear of Minerva as her needle'.[25] Yet even he, Hemans was relieved to find out, considered domesticity and genius to be accordant, as she wrote to a friend in 1830: 'You may remember how much I disliked, and I think you agreed with me in reprobating, that shallow theory of Mr Moore's with regard to the unfitness of genius for domestic happiness. I was speaking of it yesterday to Mr Wordsworth, and was pleased by his remark, "It is not because they *possess* genius that they make unhappy homes, but because they do not possess genius *enough*; a higher order of mind would enable them to see and feel all the beauty of domestic ties" '.[26]

This early poem, however, was influenced less by Wordsworth than by Shelley, who, as Gary Kelly tells us, had written to the young Felicia Browne after reading *England and Spain* (1808) to 'dissuade her from support for war and a belief in God'.[27] Arguably the poem asserts an anti-war agenda anyway, prefiguring the call for peace forwarded in 'The Domestic Affections' (1812) through what Kelly calls a 'domestic ideology', thoughtful, emotive, liberal and religious. 'Fields of carnage' may threaten this ideology, Hemans writes, but it is 'that lov'd home, where pure affection glows' that serves as war's counter, the only place able to 'cheer the soldier's breast' (ll. 113, 115, 121). Only here may true solace be found:

> Bower of repose! when torn from all we love,
> Through toil we struggle, or through distance rove;
> To *thee* we turn, still faithful, from afar,
> Thee, our bright vista! thee, our magnet-star!
> And from the martial field, the troubled sea,
> Unfetter'd thought still roves to bliss and thee!
>
> (ll. 77–82)

For Hemans, the 'sweet endearments of domestic ties' are authenticated by heaven through 'angel sympathies!' and illuminated by the individual's own investment in such a realm as a place in which one's thoughts, and hence feelings, are 'unfetter'd' (ll. 82, 153–4). The freedom to think and feel through affection was paramount for the poet, a process enabled and reproduced by and within the home. While later poems like 'The Forsaken Hearth' (1828) and 'The Voice of Home to the Prodigal' (1828) would express Hemans's anxieties regarding the demise of the home, here she raises it up as a symbolic, rather than material, space in which virtue, morality and feeling can be learned and explored. Hemans believed from a very early age that the best way of communicating these values was poetry, and 'The Domestic Affections', with its 'Arcadian bowers' and musical rhythms, advocates the lyric as Wordsworth's famous Preface had done a decade earlier. The 'fairy scene' of the home is made magical, then, by the poetry that builds and constructs it, just as verse had been a vital genre for the religious dissenters who had established the liberal and cosmopolitan Enlightenment values that flourished in Liverpool and elsewhere.

RADICAL POETRY

Hemans was familiar with the radical potential of poetry, not only from her acquaintance with the works of Coleridge, Wordsworth and Byron, but also because of the Liverpool scene that surrounded her, headed by the reform campaigner, William Roscoe. Roscoe was close friends with the publisher Joseph Johnson, whose London circle comprised many politically active poets, and his son helped publish some of Hemans's early works. Like Wordsworth, Hemans recognized poetry as an overflow of feeling, but she believed the dissemination of such feeling through the lyric would soften society, easing political strife, diminishing support for war and encouraging a shared sense of respect between the sexes. Thus, for her, the arousal of emotion in her readers was a political move. As Ross suggests: 'There is no doubt that Hemans sees her goal as the feminisation of culture at large. Bringing her readers to tears is not simply a way of sensitising them individually; it is more importantly a way of transforming them collectively into a community of shared desire.'[28] Kelly concurs with Ross in his own argument about Hemans's role in the formation of a modern liberal state, her poetry, he asserts, confirming the 'values, knowledge and outlook of what was at that time the revolutionary class' and addressing the changing culture in which her reading public was immersed.[29] Both a domestic poet of the household and a public speaker on issues of national import, Hemans assumed for herself 'the role of model liberal subject', Kelly suggests, an example that two major shaping forces of the nineteenth-century liberal state, William Gladstone and Robert Peel, would intently follow. Gladstone credited his moral and religious education to Hemans's poetry; while Peel felt it a 'public duty' and 'honour' to offer the poet £100 and a government job for her son when he 'heard from an authority' that she was 'suffering from sickness'.[30]

No wonder Hemans felt the status of poet to be one of power and profound responsibility. As Hughes wrote of her sister's *New Monthly Magazine* article on Goethe's dramatic poem *Torquato Tasso* (1790): 'it embodies' her 'feeling with respect to the high and sacred mission of the Poet; as well as regarding that mysterious analogy between the outer world of nature and the inner world of the heart'.[31] As Hemans confirmed, the poet assumes a 'high office' when he or she speaks lyrically, duty-bound to mould 'from the sorrows, the affections, the fiery trials, and immortal longings of the human soul' a poetry that rings with 'the tones of prayer' and 'the suffering spirit – *there* lie his veins of treasure'.[32] Yet being a poet was increasingly questionable during the nineteenth century, the genre steadily overtaken by a growing interest in prose, journalistic and novelistic alike. In a letter dated 1831, Hemans was forced to admit: 'Certainly poetry is a mere "waif and stray" in this work-day world of ours'.[33] As the discontinuity between aesthetic and other experiences became more pronounced, lyric was associated with pastoral solitude and religious retreat. Reviewing Coleridge's *Biographia Literaria* (1817), Hazlitt firmly asserted: 'We would not, with Plato, absolutely banish poets from the commonwealth; but we really think they should meddle as little with its practical administration as may be. They live in an ideal world of their own; and it would be well, if they were confined to it.'[34] Moreover, as Douglas Lane Patey suggests, the realm of poetry began to 'exclude erudition and participation in practical affairs' and evoke instead feeling without judgement, and sentiment without thought.[35] Armed with the fusion of thought and feeling the affections provided, Hemans sought to return the lyric to an earlier mode in which narrators served as models for readers and where, as Edward Young wrote, what 'comes from [the poet's] head sets our brains at work, and our hearts at ease', making 'a circle of thoughtful critics'.[36] Like Young, Hemans aspired to produce a christianizing poetry which will be discussed later. Here it is enough to focus on her elevation of the lyric as the most beneficial, and therefore radical, of all genres to the reader's mind and soul, a mantra that she successfully communicated to her ever-growing readership.

No doubt Hemans made money by writing poetry. Paula Feldman has revealed not only that Hemans was the highest paid contributor to *Blackwood's Magazine*, rated above Scott, Godwin and De Quincey, but also that she was able to negotiate successfully the literary marketplace with her contributions to the annuals.[37] Yet the poet was careful to align herself with the lyric tradition which, as noted in the introduction, framed the beauty of poetical production with sincere feeling and sorrow. From 'Address to the Deity', written when she was only 11, Hemans searched for an external power that would augment her internal feelings and so enhance her capabilities as a lyric poet. She thus invokes God 'To swell the adoration of the lyre', entreating him as the 'Source of all good' to 'oh! teach my voice to sing' (ll. 2–3). Lyric was an ideal genre for communicating feeling because, unlike narrative and dramatic poetry, it retained a musical expression that lifted the reader out of the discursive and into emotion. Barbara Hardy argues that it is because the lyric 'does not provide an explanation, judgement or narrative' that it can express 'concentrated' feeling: ideas, subjects, characters and themes might be present in the lyric, but 'they are marshalled in the service of feeling'.[38] Part of the lyric's power, then, is that it excises explanations and contexts to allow the narrator fully to expel and to explore his or her feelings and so amplify them, making, Hardy suggests, 'feeling public even as it preserves a privacy in declining to furnish attendant circumstances'.[39] Both public and private, lyric suited Hemans's at once civic and domestic voice, and championed feeling as that which comprises reason and thought as well as emotion. As Hemans's contemporary, August Schlegel, declared: '*Feeling* perceives all in all at one and the same time', an expression of Romanticism, he argued, as opposed to Classicism.[40] Hemans told Chorley that she preferred Romantic to classic poetry, being far more an affective lyrist than an Enlightenment versifier, and in a letter written in 1828 she damned 'those hateful engines, commonly called the "reasoning powers"'.[41] If, as Adorno and Horkeimer would later maintain, 'the program of the Enlightenment was the disenchantment of the world', Hemans believed poetry to be a mode of re-enchantment, lulling her readers into a receptively emotional state.[42]

How insightful, then, was Maria Jane Jewsbury when she claimed of her friend: 'It was poetry that she sought in history, scenery, character and religious belief, – poetry that guided all her studies, governed all her thoughts, coloured all her conversation'.[43] Even her plays read as closet dramas, more privately lyrical than performative. The literary journals too recognized and supported Hemans's lyrical project. As the *Edinburgh Monthly Review* exclaimed in 1819, reviewing *Tales, and Historic Scenes*: 'Every one knows the recent remarkable history of poetry, and its present actual predicament [. . .] Never was more poetry written, and less poetry read. The multitude have had enough. The enthusiasm which has now cooled was founded on exhaustible feelings.' Yet, the reviewer continues, 'if the multitude neglect' Mrs Hemans, and push 'off to novels', they will miss the ventures of a writer who 'excites emotion which endures, and which gives fresh delight on repetition, by expressing natural feeling, in a sweet flow of tenderness, or a sustained and deep tone of pathos'.[44] Notably, the review highlights Hemans's predilection for the communication of fervent emotion through the lyric, but such a strategy is not absolutely bound to gender at this point in her career. Arguably, she is only 'feminized' around the time of the publication of *Records of Woman* (1828), and until then maintains an ardent, yet resoundingly political, pitch, tuned primarily to the subject of nation.

NATION AND PATRIOTISM

Nation was an enduring topic for Hemans, and Tricia Lootens claims that her poetic career was almost uniquely invested in the 'construction of national identity'.[45] Hemans versified on nation in two central ways: first, by focusing on war, addressing discourses of patriotism, chivalry and military glory; and second, by examining and extolling the role of culture and art in the construction of all nations. Her war poetry in particular has touched the nerve of many modern critics, who have found her allegiance to the 'British' nation both naïve and offensive. Yet Hemans was not a patriot in a conventional sense, her various verses on the Greeks, Germans, Moors, Norwegians, Spaniards and Welsh revealing an interest in different kinds of nation rather than an impulse to contain all nationalities within a British framework.[46] The move to render Hemans the voice of the British battle cry is rooted in the popularity of her well-known 'Casabianca' (1826), which charts the unnecessary death of a young boy caught in the Battle of the Nile. Remaining at his post on board a burning ship commanded by his father, now unconscious, Casabianca extols an ambivalent sense of duty that highlights both the inanity of war and the honour of patriotic martyrdom: 'beautiful and bright he stood,/ As born to rule the storm;/ A creature of heroic blood,/ A proud, though child-like form' (ll. 5–8). These lines, however, are immediately countered by an expression of the futility of patriarchal and militaristic law: 'The flames roll'd on – he would not go/ Without his Father's word' (ll. 9–10). The closing couplet, 'the noblest thing which perish'd there/ Was that young faithful heart', may ostensibly uphold family duty and national honour, but it also suggests that the consequences of war are the destruction of youth, faith and nobility, a high price for the elevation of nationalism. Many of her militaristic poems express similarly fragmented representations of war, seeming to glorify its cause and yet pulling back from such glorification in the wake of death and loss. As Lootens notes, 'War and Peace: A Poem', 'The Battle Field' and even the public-spirited 'English Soldier's Song of Memory' foreshadow Rupert Brooke – and yet, as a woman, Hemans remains on the margins of conflict as she suffers from the desolation that ensues. The notion that she was candidly 'extolling the virtues of dashing soldiers' and 'marrying them' is not only problematic in light of her husband's early desertion of her, but also because it fails to recognize the layers of anti-war sentiment that thread through even her most rallying of war poems.[47]

The combative aspects of nation were not as explicit in Hemans's poetry as the cultural formation of such a unit: the nation, like the poet, is viewed as responsible for producing moral and affectionate subjects. For Hemans, as we have seen, the poet's role in society was radically pedagogic – moralizing, christianizing and rendering emotive and thoughtful his or her readers. Such a role could only be enabled by a nation invested in culture, aesthetics and art, and, in turn, its now civilized subjects had to contribute to the ongoing process of re-culturing the nation. As Isobel Armstrong points out, however, there is a contradiction at play here, the aesthetic at once presented as an 'autonomous, transnational space in civil society' and as 'a specific political achievement of the nation state'.[48] Hemans negotiates this by offering her British readership examples of how to, and how not to, construct their nation, in two successive poems, *The Restoration of the Works of Art to Italy* (1816) and *Modern Greece* (1817). *The Restoration* addresses Napoleon's plundering of around five thousand artworks during his campaigns, and the subsequent return of this art after his fall in 1815. Like de Staël's heroine, Corinne, Hemans celebrates an independent Italy which, as Armstrong suggests, is seen to deserve its art objects back because of their origins in 'sacred earth': Italy, where christianity flourished and spread, is confirmed by religious art, that which 'Pourtrays' the nation 'ineffably divine' (ll. 502). *Modern Greece*, however, suggests that this newly forged state has no claim upon stolen artworks, notably the Parthenon marbles taken by Lord Elgin to London, and instead laments the passing of that model civilized nation state, ancient Greece. Comparing the poems brings us back to Hemans's constant revaluation of lyrical feeling: Greece is depicted through images of conflict, despair and delirium, while Italy is rendered sublime, gleaming, ecstatic and a place where 'loftiest feelings glow', 'Land of the lyre!'[49] As she states in the Preface to her translation of six Italian sonnets, *Patriotic Effusions of the Italian Poets* (1821), the truly 'affecting' heights of 'high-toned feeling' are only reached when a 'patriotic chord is struck', one that rings through readers so that they cannot fail to 'sympathise with the emotions of a modern Roman, surrounded by the ruins of the Capitol; a Venetian, when contemplating the proud trophies won by his ancestors at Byzantium, or a Florentine amongst the tombs of the mighty dead, in the church of Santa Croce'.[50]

Hemans was also fascinated by Spain's status as a christian nation as well as its alliance with Britain against France in the Peninsular campaign which she celebrated as a mark of chivalric revival. 'The Noble Spaniards!', she wrote to her aunt in 1808, 'surely, surely, they will be crowned with success [. . .] you know not what an enthusiast I am in the cause of Castile and liberty: my whole heart and soul are interested for the gallant patriots'.[51] Some fifteen years later, Hemans recalled this adolescent fervour, writing that the events of the war 'are so associated in my mind with the most vivid recollections of my early youth that I could almost fancy I had passed that period of my life in the days of Chivalry, so high and ardent were the feelings they excited'.[52] The emphasis on chivalry here is in part a response to Burke's reflections on the cruel treatment of Marie Antoinette by the apparently 'gallant nation' of France: 'I thought ten thousand swords must have leaped from their scabbards to avenge even a look that threatened her with insult', he miserably wrote, 'But the age of chivalry is gone'.[53] Certainly the poet idealized Spain's national icon, El Cid, an aristocratic warrior-hero born around 1043 and, despite the historical realities of his fickle political affiliations, rendered a saint after his death. The chivalric hero of christian Castile, El Cid was a figure of fascination in the Romantic era, heralding not only a modish antiquarian and medieval aura, represented by Southey's *Chronicle of the Cid* (1808); but also a contemporary insight into Britain's sympathy for Spain's anti-Napoleonic nationalism. When Wellington negotiated the Convention of Cintra in 1808, liberating Lisbon by transporting the French army back to France, many British writers, Hemans, Wordsworth and Byron among them, considered Spain's valour betrayed. The conflict in Spain quickly crumbled into a civil war wherein the French monarchy was restored. Amidst the collapsed hope that ensued, Hemans began work on her dramatic work *The Siege of Valencia* (1823). The poem's narrative is set in an imaginary thirteenth-century Moorish siege of the christian Valencia, which is governed by a descendant of El Cid, Gonzalez, and his wife, Elmina. Their two sons are captured by the Moors, who demand the surrender of the city as ransom; Gonzalez refuses, encouraging his wife to accept the glorious martyrdom of the boys. Elmina dissents from his decision, however, much to the anger of the city, and she enters the Moors' camp in male disguise in a clandestine and ultimately vain attempt to save the brothers. When the elder is slain, Gonzalez throws himself into battle only to receive a fatal wound. The poem ends with his noble funeral, Valencia saved at the last moment by the King of Castile's christian army.

The poem turns on the figure of Elmina who is presented as the most humane of the players, bravely undertaking to save her boys even while threatened by both the anger of those at home and the wrath of the Moors. Reflecting on the poem through the events of 11 September 2001, Susan Wolfson and Elizabeth Fay argue that 'Hemans's imaginative power is to push patriotic rallying to a radical but implicitly logical consequence – the martyrdom of children in filial obedience to fathers, domestic, national, and religious – and to stage this consequence in ways that put pressure on the whole system.'[54] This pressure in fact exploded a system that tied chivalry and religion to war and power: chivalry, like faith, may be twisted to serve false causes, but at root signified a sense of valour and manners that would contribute to the production of an affectionate nation. The material action associated with chivalry, namely combat, is not at issue here: the *Siege*, like her *Songs of the Cid* (1823) and *The Forest Sanctuary* (1825), blatantly betrays the bitter despair that comes from aggression, conflict and dominance. Rather, it is the values behind chivalry – christian and courtly – that both attracted and engaged Hemans as a poet. David Rothstein suggests that Hemans reconfigured chivalrous values to accord with a domesticated, gendered and orthodox religious perspective in which conservative notions of femininity and class are underlined.[55] The emotional forces that Rothstein argues give form to national fantasies of social hierarchies and masculine heroism might also be understood, however, as fuelling a more radical notion of feeling. Her feminine revision of historical chivalry illuminates not the glory of war but instead the affectionate bonds one might forge with a fellow citizen under the banner of christianity.

Hemans's ideal nation, then, was made up of private individuals of both sexes who related to one another in a communal, public sense: feminine, christian, domestic, chivalric and emotive. Religion's profoundly intimate attention to the individual became for Hemans, like Wordsworth, a more general valuing of people that would extend into an understanding of all subjects and subject positions. As Madame de Staël argued in her study of nation, *A Treatise on the Influence of the Passions* (1798), religion is an inextricable part of any communal formation in this period, one which has 'exhibited the most striking proofs of the power and influence of religion'.[56] It is the inherent passion of religion, however, that for de Staël binds it to chivalry and romance, each furnishing 'a code' of responsibility towards others and so promoting a way of 'continuing to love'.[57] Love is at the centre of Hemans's concentration on states of feeling, whatever subject or historical age she is addressing, and is often what gives her poetry the 'glassy surface' on which readers slip and slide, finding no hook on which to hang critical readings.[58] Her nation poetry often avoids the critical char of the brand 'gushiness', but it is still deemed dubiously emotive because 'obsessed with gender'.[59] As Richard Cronin asserts, Hemans defines and valorizes the feminine only in relation to the masculine, leaving both subject positions open to men and women alike. In the *Siege*, Elmina must wear male attire to enter the Moors' camp and, when she finds her sons, the younger is overtly feminized in comparison with his older, virile brother: the former longs for reunion with his mother while the heir to Gonzalez's rule exudes a robust, if insipid, commitment to the idea of noble death. Hemans herself was occasionally regarded as a 'manly' and political writer although she clearly privileged femininity as the identity most suited to marshalling her affectionate and christian worldview.[60] As Elmina revealingly declares, surrounded by Castilian knights, the 'sound of triumphant music' and the dying gasps of her controlling, patriarchal husband: 'Now is my life uprooted, – and 'tis well' (l. 202).

FEMININITY

Mary Russell Mitford said of Hemans, 'she always does seem to me a lady rather than a woman'.[61] This was the general consensus about the poet throughout the nineteenth century, Harriet Hughes rendering her sister 'intensely feminine', William Michael Rossetti also finding 'the tone of her mind feminine in an intense degree', Symons believing that she 'had all the feminine accomplishments of her time' and Courtney heralding her 'sensitive femininity' as the triumph of her poetic project.[62] Rowton is perhaps most effusive on this subject, arguing that Hemans seemed 'to represent and unite as purely and completely as any other writer in our literature the peculiar and specific qualities of the female mind. Her works are to my mind a perfect embodiment of woman's soul: – I would say that they are *intensely* feminine. The delicacy, the softness, the pureness, the quick observant vision, the ready sensibility, the devotedness, the faith of woman's nature find in Mrs Hemans their ultra representative.'[63] Rose Lawrence even claimed that the task of writing Hemans's memoirs was 'only for a woman's hand'.[64] While Rossetti would later argue that 'feminine' had come to signify 'weakness' in literary style, Hemans's femininity signalled her genius for early- to mid-nineteenth-century readers.[65] There were some who found this problematic, of course, unable to reconcile her literary ability with her femininity: Wordsworth, as we have noted, was perplexed by Hemans's lack of housewifely skill and Byron wrote to their mutual publisher, John Murray, of 'your feminine *He-Man*' and 'Mrs Hewomans'.[66] Maria Jane Jewsbury, however, praised her friend's femininity by depicting her in the graceful character of Egeria in 'The History of a Nonchalant' (1830), a woman whom she describes as 'totally different from any other woman I had ever seen, either in Italy or England. She did not dazzle, she subdued me. Other women might be more commanding, more versatile, more acute; but I never saw one so exquisitely feminine. [. . .] Her birth, her education, but above all, the genius with which she was gifted, combined to inspire a passion for the ethereal, the tender, the imaginative, the heroic, – in one word, the beautiful. It was in her a faculty divine, and yet of daily life – it touched all things.'[67]

Jewsbury's portrayal of Hemans accords with what contemporary readers believed her to be: ethereal and intellectual, heroic (or patriotic) and imaginative, religious and domestic. Further, Jewsbury intimates that in the figure of Hemans was a new phenomenon in women's poetry, diverging from Italianate and English models of female poets. The reference to Italian women registers the model provided for women poets by de Staël's doomed heroine, Corinne, Landon and Barrett Browning famously basing passages of their own work on Corinne's lyrical improvisations. The English women poets to which Jewsbury alludes fell into a further two separate groups: the so-called 'bluestockings', who were associated with a type of Wollstonecraftian intellectualism; and the Della Cruscans, briefly popular for their violent, but assumed superficial, expression of romantic suffering and anguish. Harriet Hughes also believed her sister to be above both labels, declaring that Hemans sought to 'counter' both 'the idea she was a *bas bleu*' and that she had ever 'saluted in some such strain of hyperbole as used to prevail in the Della Cruscan coteries'.[68] Hemans's writing was most likely a product of all these traditions, and the poet illustrated her awareness of them in poems like 'Corinna at the Capitol', which cleverly recalls not only de Staël's novel and a bluestocking interest in classicism, but also Byron's forays into Della Cruscan poetics. As Susan Wolfson shows, the poem is layered with references, both to de Staël's female laureate and to Corinna, the Boetian poet of Greek antiquity reported to have prevailed over Pindar five times for the lyric prize.[69] This 'Daughter of th' Italian heaven!' is celebrated here for 'O'er three hundred triumphs gone' (ll. 1, 6), a reference, as Hemans's own footnote attests, to Byron's depiction of a ruined Rome in *Childe Harold* (1812–18), once associated with 'The trebly hundred triumphs!' but now fallen into 'decay' (Canto IV, stanza lxxxii). Wolfson argues that while Hemans might have compared Corinna to Byron's resurrection of Rome in his poem, she chooses instead to identify her with Rome's ruin, the final message of the poem being that women who wear the 'laurel' risk jettisoning their domestic security (l. 46). Moreover, such a sentiment underlines the poem's epigraph from de Staël's *Influence of the Passions*, in which women are warned that the poetical career pales in comparison to 'the most obscure life of a beloved wife and a happy mother'.[70]

Records of Woman (1828) clearly evinces Jewsbury and Hughes's promotion of Hemans's new kind of poetical voice as one able to rework trends in women's poetry. The nineteen poems that make up *Records* prefaced thirty-eight miscellaneous poems and serve to position Hemans as a powerful poetic voice in dialogue with other leading Romantic figures, the volume introduced by epigraphs from Wordsworth and Schiller while quoting extensively from Byron. Yet, importantly, *Records* was dedicated to Joanna Baillie, whose tragedy *The Family Legend* (1810) had offered Hemans a new perspective on female heroines. In a letter dated May 15, 1823, she writes of Baillie's play:

> I was much pleased by her delineation of the heroine. Indeed, nothing in all her writings delights me as much as her general idea of what is beautiful in the female character. There is so much gentle fortitude, and deep self-devoting affection in the women whom she portrays, and they are so perfectly different from the pretty 'un-idea'd' girls who seem to form the beau ideal of our whole sex in the works of some modern poets. The latter remind me of a foolish saying, I think of Diderot's, that in order to describe a woman, you should write with a pen made of a peacock's feather, and dry the writing with the dust from butterflies' wings.[71]

When Hemans described women, then, she took care not to sentimentalize, but neither did she forge them in a classical guise. While her speakers are in part based on Schiller's spirited heroines who obey their own wills and break from the domestic sphere, few relinquish domestic feeling, invested as they are in using it to personalize and feminize their narratives.[72] 'The Memorial Pillar', for example, written shortly after the death of Hemans's own mother, takes its title from a monument erected by a daughter for her mother in 1616. Feminizing history by focusing on a private moment rather than a public incident, the speaker finds comfort in their union in death: 'Mother and child! – Your tears are past –/ Surely your hearts have met at last!' (ll. 59–60). Like the framing epigraph from Schiller, taken from a monologue which mourns the doomed destiny of female emotion outside of the heavenly realm, Hemans continually emphasizes the fragility of human love when compared to religious feeling.[73] Yet these poems also force their female protagonists to confront directly the problems from which they suffer on earth, conveying such trauma through the figurative language of the lyric which standardizes the experience presented. As Virginia Jackson and Yopie Prins declare, the lyric allowed Hemans to 'imagine the terms of subjectivity' as 'generic', and so to attribute the pathos of woman's plight to an 'outside position' rather than to her own private self.[74]

At the same time, the characters created in *Records* emotionally recall genuine instances of women's experience in the world, the very word 'record', as Kelly reminds us, coming from the Latin cor/cordis for heart and so symbolizing an authorial sympathy Hemans expected her readers to emulate.[75] That Hemans offered readers records of emotion rather than grandiose historical events casts a different light over her re-creation of the past in her poetry, one that seems to invoke cultural nostalgia even as it reconfigures the moments on which this is based. Thus her poetical snapshots of a medieval, aristocratic and chivalric tradition are often revisionary, fostering in the reader an awareness of class, gender and religious ideology. The opening poem in Records, 'Arabella Stuart', exemplifies this by taking the tragic story of the eldest daughter of Henry VII and recounting it as a lyric poem spoken by Stuart herself. While the reader is made aware of such revisions through a historical prose preface, even this makes explicit that Stuart's 'domestic happiness' was crushed by her affinity to the public sphere of the throne and monarchy, one which resulted in the disciplining of all her romantic attachments. Commonly thought to have sunk into insanity after the failure of a secret attempt to escape abroad with her lover, William Seymour, Stuart is rendered, if not mad, emotionally broken by circumstance, a victim of the king's panoptical control and of Seymour's cowardice. Thrown into prison for her treason, Stuart effuses more than just a personal statement of sadness, however, drawing attention to both the cruelty of sovereign control, 'some dark watchful power,' and the penalty of being an independent woman (l. 22). Again, only heaven provides a safe-haven when domestic security is removed, a location in which women can be fervent without retribution:

> And feeling still my woman's spirit strong,
> In the deep faith which lifts from earthly wrong,
> A heavenward glance.

(ll. 32–4)

The poem becomes prayer here, only God welcoming the woman of feeling in all her fervent emotional and sexual longing: 'Father in Heaven!', Stuart cries, 'Thou, only thou, canst sound/ The heart's great deep, with floods of anguish fill'd' (ll. 213–14). For the happiness Seymour offered is betrayed as a prize 'bought with burning tears!' a phrase that indicates the material transaction that romance becomes for women as they risk losing status, wealth and freedom (l. 257). Stuart's belief that the weight of her emotion might find expression only in the 'holy place' of her lover's heart indicates a popular theme within the *Records*: secular love always enhanced and upstaged by the sacred (l. 265).

'Joan of Arc, in Rheims' mirrors the preoccupations of 'Arabella Stuart', and yet is written as a commentary rather than personal prayer. Like Stuart, Joan is pictured gazing upwards 'Intensely worshipping': God is able to embrace a 'woman, mantled with victorious power' even as society cannot (ll. 23, 36). Hemans honours the military leader in the morally upright and religiously orthodox tones of Arthurian legend, 'Holy amidst the knighthood of the land' (l. 38). Yet this chivalrous image of the cross-dressed soldier is countered by an emphasis upon her beauty and grace, the 'warlike melodies' that frame the first half of the poem set against the later invocation of childhood memories which invariably win Joan 'back to nature' (ll. 48, 82). Her 'high career' and 'fame', like Stuart's transitory joy with Seymour, come at a cost, the narrator concludes, 'bought alone by gifts beyond all price', and threatening to block access to 'the paradise/ Of home' (ll. 53, 91–5). The association of 'paradise' with 'home' lifts the latter above the drudgery of the merely domestic, both 'Joan of Arc' and 'Arabella Stuart' attributing the lack of intellectual and emotional freedom from which women suffer to the petty and yet devastating social codes that structured middle-class society. As Chorley wryly commented regarding Hemans's politely dull female acquaintances in Wavertree, they come to 'pay proper neighbourly morning calls, and discuss household matters. Great was their surprise at finding that she was not ready with an answer on these important topics.'[76]

Hemans's frustration with bourgeois civility was that it resisted the expression of fierce emotion and so threatened the media through which such feeling had an outlet, notably art and poetry. 'Properzia Rossi' is a brilliant vindication of emotion, the spurned sculptor Rossi carving an image of Ariadne before she dies, in the hope that she might evoke feeling in the lover who has rejected her. The affections are key to the poem, and their centrality is made all the more apparent by the fact that they are not present in the absent lover. That combination of feeling and thought is represented by – indeed, cast within – the statue, leaving 'enshrined', as the narrator expresses it, something immortal:

> May this last work, this farewell triumph be –
> Thou, loved so vainly! I would leave enshrined
> Something immortal of my heart and mind
> That yet may speak to thee when I am gone,
> Shaking thine inmost bosom with a tone
> Of lost affection.

(ll. 8–13)

Recreating herself in the statue, Rossi celebrates her aesthetic skill, fixing her 'thought, heart, soul, to burn, to shine' within the 'marble's veins' to make tangible the pulsating force that enables the 'bright work' to grow (ll. 33, 36–7). 'Thou art the mould/ Wherein I pour the fervent thoughts', she declares to her creation, its very being a record of her 'burning heart' which is 'kindled' only 'with the fire of heaven' (ll. 45–6, 63, 67). Again, heaven is the sole receptacle of 'deep affections, that o'erflow', the statue's ultimate 'unchange'd' form ossifying those feelings that only live on within religious realms. Yet such realms include the lyric itself, that form which is fuelled by feeling, outliving the narrator and the crumbling statue alike and standing firm in its role as a vehicle for religious feeling. As Rossi declares, 'a deep thrill may linger on the lyre' even 'When its full chords are hush'd', an avowal of poetry's strength in reinforcing female artistic power even when it is silenced (ll. 126–7).

RELIGION

Apparent throughout this chapter has been Hemans's emphasis upon lyric form, whether as a radical genre, or as an ideal container for strong feeling that is released by the poet's voice. This strong feeling can be read as religious, as we found in some of the *Records*, but Hemans sometimes refers to a more specific kind of religious feeling called 'affection'. Historically, the 'affections' signified a less violent and sensuous set of emotions than that which the 'passions' designated, a rational sentiment that became popular with British moralists like Shaftesbury and Adam Smith. Within their writings, affection appeared as a social force at the heart of civic identity, heightening within us feelings of benevolence, sympathy and morality.[77] Theologians also stressed the rational side of the affections, William Fenner describing them in *A Treatise of the Affections; or the Soules Pulse* (1641) as inherent to the will and separate from unreasonable feeling, like passion or enthusiasm.[78] Francis Hutcheson concurred in his *Essay on the Nature and Conduct of the Passions and Affections* (1728), in which he wrote that 'Affections' were spiritualized, gentle feelings focused upon the purity of God.[79] During the eighteenth century, preachers like Isaac Watts and Jonathan Edwards claimed the affections as specifically religious in tone, contending that they were the only kind of feelings that could channel both the 'imagination' and the 'heart' into 'devotion to God'.[80] To comprehend God truly, Watts argued, reason must be balanced by the affections within the believer, 'the light of nature and reason' a 'poor dark bewildered thing' without them.[81] Registering a religious feeling that allowed the individual to approach God through both the mind and the heart, feeling and thinking about him simultaneously, affection enabled the individual to believe in God as 'true' while also feeling his being within faith. Hemans found affection even more attractive as a type of feeling open to women, who were considered the guardians of this christianized sensibility. If affection fused feeling and thought, then the lyric provided the ideal stage for its performance, its form able to create an experiential space wherein intense feeling might be profoundly felt and thought about.

This definition of affection is attested to in the reviews of Hemans's first major religious lyric, 'The Sceptic' (1820), which invited the reader to consider, feel and ultimately reject the despair that issues from religious doubt and unbelief. The *Edinburgh Monthly Review* praised Hemans's fusion of a 'vigorous intellect' and 'warm and confiding piety' in the poem, one which produced a 'divine and mysterious vigour' readers could employ in their own responses to religion.[82] As the

Quarterly Review noted, the poem expressed an 'irresistible force' able to 'confirm a wavering mind', appealing to both 'the imagination and passions of man'.[83] This emphasis upon 'The Sceptic's ability to exude an energy that had the capacity to penetrate readers' hearts and minds falls closely in line with the concept of affection, and Charles Eliot Norton even considered the poem a study of how 'unbelief' impacts on 'the affections and gentler part of our nature'.[84] The poem may be read as an attack on the ostensible scepticism made popular in narratives like Byron's *Manfred* (1817), in which the Faustian hero denies the power of all spiritual aid at his peril. Finding beauty only 'in all this visible world!' rather than in the unseen realms of faith, Manfred expresses envy toward an eagle soaring overhead, a 'winged and cloud-cleaving minister,/ Whose happy flight is highest into heaven' (ll. 291–2, 298). Responding to Manfred's incapacity to envision his own 'flight' to heaven, Hemans begins 'The Sceptic' with a parallel image of an eagle:

> Will his free wing, from that majestic height,
> Descend to follow some wild meteor's light,
> Which, far below, with evanescent fire,
> Shines to delude, and dazzles to expire?
> No!
>
> (ll. 5–9)

Hemans's eagle follows not the 'earth-born light' of fire nor the meteoric flash of space, but relies instead on a religious light which cannot be extinguished (l. 14). The poem encourages readers to align themselves symbolically with the eagle's trajectory, choosing an immaterial, spiritual and anti-rational way of living embraced by faith rather than suspicion. Freeing oneself from the binds of logic and intellectual rationality, the subject might then protect him- or herself against disappointment, anguish and broken love. How 'canst thou dare to *love*?' the narrator wonders, without God's invisible direction, 'thou whose thoughts have no blest home above' any more than a 'Captive of earth' (ll. 71–2). While 'unseen', God reveals himself to the believer by investing his power within human emotion and its expression in poetry (l. 100). Pervading 'the living lyre', God is himself revealed within the 'deep chords'

40

of verse, the 'mighty harmony' within waking 'each passion from its cell profound' as 'nations start at the electric sound' (ll. 249–54). Arousing passion and feeling within us, God finds the outlet he needs to convince sceptics, Hemans argues, and the encouragement of an emotional sensitivity within her readership becomes an objective she believes only religious poetry can achieve.

Certainly Hemans believed she had a role to play in the creation of a public climate that would be receptive to warm religious feeling, *Songs of the Affections* (1830), *Female Characters of Scripture* (1833), *Sonnets, Devotional and Memorial* (1833) and *Scenes and Hymns of Life* (1834) all testifying to her spiritual concerns.[85] The *Athenaeum* even identified the 'fountain and principle of her inspirations' as a type of 'Honour deepened and sanctified by religion' and depicted by her creation of 'a world of high-souled men and women'.[86] Hemans's own religious beliefs had been shaped by the pedagogical influences of Bishop Reginald Heber, William Channing, Blanco White and Archbishop Whately, and she had developed spiritually through acquaintance with Hannah More, Walter Scott, Baillie and Wordsworth.[87] She had also encountered several different belief systems during her life: a politicized Anglicanism in Liverpool; Low Church nonconformism at Rhyllon, where she lived in the 1820s; and Roman Catholicism during her residence in Ireland from 1831. Arguably, most of Hemans's poetry is 'religious', emitting a numinous feeling that is rooted in affection; but some of her verse, such as the unfinished 'Superstition and Revelation' (*c.* 1820), more specifically addresses questions about christianity. Hemans declared in 1820 that this poem was written to contrast 'the spirit and tenets of Paganism with those of Christianity', but she abandoned the project after receiving Heber's Tory and religiously orthodox critique of an early draft. As Nanora Sweet argues, the poem manifests a liberal, sometimes Unitarian and often Shelleyan syncretism which is at odds with Heber's Oxford Anglicanism. The opening stanza attempts almost to harmonize spiritualism and established religion:[88]

> Beings of brighter worlds! that rise at times
> As phantoms, with ideal beauty fraught,

In those brief visions of celestial climes,
Which pass, like sunbeams, o'er the realms of thought,
Dwell ye around us? – are ye hovering nigh,
Throned on the cloud, or buoyant in the air?
And in deep solitudes, where human eye
Can trace no step, Immortals! are ye there?
Oh! who can tell? – what power, but Death alone
Can lift the mystic veil that shades the world unknown?

(ll. 1–10)

Behind the 'mystic veil' of the final line dwell beings theogonic and christian alike, Hemans suggests, and it is her priority to identify not *who* such beings are but what kind of power or feeling they convey. Ethereal and phantom-like, these beings are as quick flashes in the dark, 'brief visions' which are glimpsed by the narrator on the level of feeling and thought: for as their glitter draws her like a magpie, she is simultaneously moved to discern what she is registering (l. 3). 'Like sunbeams' the spirits brush over her thought, sparks ignited by an unknown 'Deity' and, as it is revealed in stanza 2, underlining our inability to define all gods (ll. 4, 19–20). Hemans's refusal to pin down the precise nature of this deity provides the foundation for the promotion of a continuity between 'superstition' and 'Christianity', a blending that mirrors the fusion of feeling and thought within affection. Heber's extensive and revisionary notes on the verses attest to only the most shallow of feeling on his part, conveying a solely rational imposition of orthodoxy over Hemans's looser christianity.

Hemans's conviction that religious poetry lacked the verve necessary to sustain it, however, did not fade with her refusal to complete the poem. While she feared that readers and her fellow poets neglected the arena of religious feeling, she found in Wordsworth a promotion of overflowing feelings grounded in religious contemplation. As Chorley claimed, Wordsworth's writing provided Hemans with a 'poetical breviary', and she considered him the leading christian poet of the day, dedicating *Scenes and Hymns of Life* to him as, she explained in 1834, a 'token of affectionate veneration'.[89] She noted in a letter to Jewsbury regarding *The Excursion* (1814) that: 'I was much struck with the beauty and sublimity of some of the religious passages it contains', the 'mingled strain of exalted hope and

42

Christian resignation' speaking 'forcibly' to 'the heart'.[90] Her residence with Wordsworth during the summer of 1830 evoked some of her most tender letters, in which she describes Rydal Mount as a 'spirit land' and an 'imaged heaven' and 'Mr Wordsworth' a charming and informal companion.[91] Together they expressed a shared disappointment in secular poets like Burns and Goethe and voiced an avid admiration of the more theologically sound Schiller. Those poems which follow her visit to the Lakes rely on scripture to a greater extent than her previous work, and seem more secure in their promotion of affection within the poet, the lyric and God. While earlier poems like 'The Lyre's Lament' (1828) conveyed Hemans's anxiety that the poet must 'wake the burning soul' of the lyric alone, a sonnet such as 'The Sacred Harp', published in *Sonnets, Devotional and Memorial* (1833), deems the poet's role priest-like, God's word vibrating through the lines of the poem as communicated by its author. Only the 'Spirit of God', the narrator claims, can allow the 'harp of poesy' to

> regain
> That old victorious tone of prophet-years,
> A spell divine o'er guilt's perturbing fears.

(ll. 1–3)

The moral duty Hemans felt to christianize her society is pronounced in this intimation of guilt, lifted only by her epiphany at the end of the sonnet that the poet exudes God's glory by crystallizing it within the lyric as affection. As the narrator declares, God's 'unseen' haunting of 'those two powers by whom the harp is strung,/ Feeling and Thought!' is what rejuvenates poetical form and religious faith alike (ll. 12–13). This theme threads through many of the devotional sonnets, such as 'On a Remembered Picture of Christ', 'The Darkness of the Crucifixion' and 'Places of Worship', in which affection breaks free from within the tight lyrical parameters of the fourteen-line form.

Affection became more central in Hemans's poetry with the publication of *Songs of the Affections*, a catalogue of intensely felt lyrics that lift the reader up beyond the page into various magical realms and spirit worlds. 'To a Departed Spirit', 'The Land of Dreams' and 'The Fountain of Oblivion' each map the ethereality of immortal domains by evoking the displacement experienced by the narrator as she imagines freedom from the material. Such mapping is particularly apparent in what is the volume's crowning poem as well as Hemans's personal favourite: 'A Spirit's Return'. Here the narrator is separated from her lover by death but reunited with his spirit in a fleeting moment of passion. She is at last destroyed, however, by the thought that her capacity to feel is stifled on earth, and that, amidst the 'far sphere' of her lover, her emotions signify 'as nothing' (ll. 188–9). Flung back to her own 'faded world' after 'one full-fraught hour of heaven,' the narrator has no choice but to wait for the time when she will join the dead, 'They that breathe purer air, that feel, that know/ Things wrapt from us!' (ll. 221, 226, 248–9). Chorley recalls that Hemans wrote the poem in response to a conversation regarding 'the feelings with which the presence and the speech of a visitant from another world' would 'impress on the person so visited'. 'Mrs Hemans', he declares, 'said that she thought' that 'the person so visited must thenceforward and for ever be inevitably separated from this world and its concerns: for the soul which had once enjoyed such a strange and spiritual communion [. . .] *must* be raised, by its experience, too high for common grief again to perplex, or common joy to enliven'.[92] By producing a poetry of affection, however, one that bound the ability to feel and to know together with religious glue, the poet believed the subject might enjoy the 'strange and spiritual communion' of heaven on earth, routed through the emotions.

Hemans was afraid, however, that besides Wordsworth, few poets were wholly committed to the task of casting the religious experience as one of emotion. She publicly voiced this fear in the Preface to *Scenes and Hymns*, stating:

> I trust I shall not be accused of presumption for the endeavour which I have here made to enlarge, in some degree, the sphere of Religious Poetry, by associating with its themes more of the emotions, the affections, and even the purer imaginative enjoyments of daily life, than may have been hitherto admitted within the hallowed circle.[93]

The 'hallowed circle', the poet thought, was dominated by doctrinal or didactic verse, full of a sermonizing pulpit eloquence she found anaesthetizing: her religious verse, she claimed, would relocate feeling at its core. Its narrators are indeed a beset group, gushing forth emotive narrations addressing abandonment, lost love, troubled faith and mourning, all united in their desire for a sphere in which such cries might be registered and understood. As in the *Records*, the endpoint of these lyrics is God, and their movement towards him often follows a similar pattern: a short drama unfolds staging the specificities of the narrator's trauma; a soliloquy-like spillage of feeling issues from the central protagonist, sometimes after a distressing dialogue with a lover or relative; and just as this effusion reaches its pitch, the narrator is cut off or shifts the form of his or her lament into a closing song. Hence the title of the volume, Hemans setting up various tragic scenes that conclude with a hymn, which, unlike a complaint or lament, specifically amplifies the sense of emotion expressed throughout the lyric. Poems such as 'The Funeral Day of Sir Walter Scott' or 'Burial of an Emigrant's Child in the Forests', for example, shift the reader from the apparent subject of the lamentation into a focus on God as he who both enables mourning and ultimately evokes a stronger emotion in its place. As the lonely and tearful narrator of 'The Prayer in the Wilderness' cries: 'O Father! draw to Thee/ My lost affections back', God called on here to flick the switch within the human heart that activates its emotions (ll. 33–4).

For Hemans, affection is both stirred by God and necessary for perceiving him, granting the subject a visionary sense through which to see the world in a christianized and emotive manner. For once one penetrates the material surface of existence, a sacred connectedness of nature and being is revealed, provoking a sense of responsibility within the self for a world upon which its own being relies. Such a philosophy is apparent within 'Wood Walk and Hymn', a dialogue between a father and child that takes place on a leisurely trek into the centre of a forest. The wood is a living and breathing entity, the hikers' goal to reach the 'inmost heart/ Of the old wood', and feel there the power of God. As the two walk together, the father recites legends related to the forest: the 'quivering' 'restlessness' of the 'aspen' a result of its use in the making of Christ's cross; the 'dark-brown stains' of the woodbine the 'atoning blood' of Christ's body; and the 'star-shaped' passion flower a symbol of the crucifixion (ll. 6, 10, 13, 39, 47, 56). The narrative here is not simply typological; the young boy questions the rationality of such mystical stories and his father underlines the fact that, while they 'walk in clearer light', it is a sense of mystery and vision that remains 'Stamp'd on the reverential soul of man' (ll. 20–24). The deeper they move into the woods, the more profound becomes their emotional reaction to the 'luxury of gloom' within, and, pausing to remember the pagans who once worshipped there, the father declares: 'but *we*, my child, are here/ With God, our God, a spirit; who requires/ Heart-worship' (ll. 90–92). Invoking the child to 'clasp my hand', father and son are both spurred by the hallowed nature of the scene to recall a woodland hymn that the child sings to conclude the poem:

> Yes, lightly, softly move!
> There *is* a Power, a Presence in the woods;
> A viewless Being, that, with life and love,
> Informs the reverential solitudes.

> (128–31)

The lines recall the closing words of Wordsworth's 'Nutting' (1799) which are used as the epigraph to the poem, invoking the reader to 'Move along these shades/ In gentleness of heart; with gentle hand/ Touch – for there is a spirit in the woods' (ll. 54–6). The connection to an unseen power in both poems is physical, Wordsworth's 'touch' and Hemans's 'clasp my hand' denoting the power of spiritual feeling to forge tangible bonds between people.

Towards the end of her life, Hemans was presented with an example of the potential effect her religious poetry produced in readers. She was living in Dublin at this time, having moved there in 1831 to be near her brother, George Browne. Confined due to illness and receiving few visitors, the poet was one day called on by a stranger, her sister tells us, who 'begged earnestly to see her'.[94] The gentleman explained 'in words and tones of the deepest feeling, that the object of his visit was to acknowledge a debt of obligation' to her after reading 'The Sceptic', a poem which had awakened within him a religious 'faith and those hopes which were now more precious to him than life itself'. Hughes recalls how moved Hemans was by the stranger's 'uncontrollable gush of emotion', humbled yet delighted by the idea that her ardent religious poetry could begin to motivate those changes in society she envisioned. Up until her death, she remained concerned that the impact her verse might have on society would falter; at one point, suffering the misery of scarlet fever, she wrote of her now stifled 'wish' to 'concentrate all my mental energy in the production of some more noble and complete work' which 'might permanently take its place as the work of a British poetess'.[95] Even when dying, finally of tuberculosis, Hemans began the prologue to a work which she was to have called *The Christian Temple*, a poem whose purpose was, according to Chorley, to trace 'out the workings of passion – the struggles of human affection'. In doing so, the poet believed she would 'illustrate the insufficiency of any dispensation, save that of an all-embracing Christianity' to 'fulfil the desires' of immortals, and much of the obsessive struggle with religion that marked the experiences of the Victorians might plausibly be attributed to Hemans's influence.[96]

On her death in 1835 Hemans quickly became a 'Victorian literary monument', St Asaph's Cathedral dedicating a memorial tablet to her, and countless poets and reviewers offering devoted eulogies.[97] Mary Carpenter, for example, a Unitarian social reformer and poet, declared that her lyrical voice would continue to christianize and bond readers in a covenant of emotion: 'Still shalt thou tell/ E'en from the tomb, how warm affections swell/ In fairest hearts'.[98] Hemans predicted this would be the case in her last poem, 'Sabbath Sonnet', dictated to her brother Charles as part of the sequence *Thoughts in Sickness* (1835). Here the poet reiterates her aspiration to unite the nation through a communal religious feeling: 'How many blessed groups this hour are bending,/ Through England's primrose meadow-paths, their way/ Towards spire and tower', she exclaims (ll. 1–3). These lines invoke a familiar, if idealized, picture of Victorian Sundays, constituted by church-goers united as a congregation of poetry readers and sensitive citizens rendered benevolent through their capacity to feel. While secular readers might feel alienated by the impassioned spiritual fervour Hemans unequivocally advocated, it is perhaps worth respecting the poet's emphasis upon what Wordsworth called 'powerful feeling', and reading and studying her work as intently as critics have that of the renowned laureate.

3

Dora Greenwell

In 1863, Dora Greenwell wrote to her friend, Professor William Knight: 'I have it in me to be anything of a Christian Leigh Hunt; or would the Christian element resist and decompose the Leigh Huntian? – I think not'.[1] This is more than a throw-away remark regarding her admiration for Leigh Hunt, whom she considered, along with Elizabeth Barrett Browning, Hemans, Coleridge and Schiller, to be a fundamental influence on her thought. For her comment more significantly highlights the main issue to which Greenwell devoted her life's work, poetry and prose alike: namely, the relationship between christianity and poetry. Her Platonic dialogue, *Two Friends* (1863), is bewildered by the connections between the two, Greenwell fretting: 'I do feel, sometimes painfully, a contradiction between the brokenness of Christ and the clear perfection of Art. The glory of the Terrestrial is one, and the glory of the Celestial is another, and these stars differ.'[2]

Greenwell had been anxious about the prospect of being a poet since she was at least 26, as her commonplace book, musingly labelled 'Stray Leaves', conveys. Poetry, she feared, 'is a morbid mental condition affecting the intellectual powers, in the manner that disease acts upon the bodily ones. Mrs Hemans [. . .] used to speak of the nerves of her mind as being *unsheathed*. Still it seems somewhat degrading to so bright and precious a gift, to be looked upon but as a *brilliant disease*.'[3] At the same time, one of Greenwell's most loved Barrett Browning quotations, cited in her poetry collection *Camera Obscura* (1876), was the latter's appeal for the involvement of religion in poetry to save the genre in an age increasingly dominated by the novel. 'We want the touch of Christ's hand upon our literature', Barrett Browning wrote, 'as it touched other dead things. We want the sense of the saturation of Christ's blood upon the souls of our poets, that it may cry through them in answer to the unceasing wail of the sphynx of our humanity, expounding agony into renovation.'[4] As we have seen, the idea that poetry might restore humanity through religion is one Hemans strongly advocated, and Greenwell too believed religious writing to be a powerful implement for social and cultural change. Unlike Hemans, however, Greenwell was driven as a thinker by her interest in, and anxiety regarding, her own capacity to be at once a devout christian and an aesthetically dazzling poet.

Arguably she did neither, her religious belief too radically open and curious to be strictly 'christian', and her poetical achievements not nearly so lyrically accomplished as those Hemans published. Yet Greenwell is a profoundly engaging writer who, as her biographer Constance Maynard declared, was possibly 'the one woman theologian of the last hundred years and perhaps for long before that'.[5] Her concern to reconcile the interests of religion and art fuels the most part of her theological essays, but Greenwell was also a social commentator who protested against the slave-trade, and worked towards securing women's rights and better working conditions for the poorer classes. Angela Leighton even suggests that it was Greenwell who converted Christina Rossetti to the anti-vivisectionist cause.[6] Significantly, however, Greenwell saw herself primarily as a poet, a reflection on the contemporary status of poetry as the genre considered closest to God in style and tone. This idea was not new, as we discovered in the Introduction, but Greenwell considered it her task to underline poetry's inherent religious aspect, as her verse 'Poets' (1861) conveys. Like the dialogue in *Two Friends*, the poem quickly stages the question of the poet's right to depict a world created by a higher being than he or she can comprehend: 'whence hast thou won/ The key to the melodies vagrant that run/ and throb along Nature's strong pulse', the narrator asks (ll. 1–3). The poet's answer is that such a key is granted by God, 'who to each at His will/ From his fulness gives somewhat the yearning to still/ Of the soul', and recognizes that every 'banquet', however divine, 'needs music' (ll. 9–11, 24). Greenwell thus implies that both literature and faith could equally and at once serve God, and, in doing so, give comfort to humanity. As Maynard declares, 'she had two loves that pervaded her whole being, and the one was Human Nature, and the other was the Cross of Christ'.[7] While her maxim, 'the poet is a man who sympathises with man, the theologian is a man who sympathises with God', echoes throughout her canon, Greenwell is always working to neutralize such a dichotomy.[8] Similarly, she is remarkably forward in her written attempts to elevate God above doctrinal distinction, asking in *A Present Heaven* (1855) why there is 'so much anxiety about points of doctrine, when it is the devotion of the heart and the practice of the life, upon which God has made salvation to depend'.[9]

The first section of this chapter will turn to the question of how Greenwell 'practised the life' she believed God had assigned to her, and explore some of the social issues to which she dedicated herself. While the association of religion and poetry inflected her less aesthetic concerns, the relationship is more prominently flagged up in a discussion of Greenwell's artistic preoccupations. Here, Greenwell's intellectual relationships will be at the fore, both with living thinkers, such as the prolific moral philosopher William Knight, and with those English and German Romantic figures that had so strikingly moved Hemans a generation earlier. Exploring such relationships leads the reader to Greenwell's controversial arguments regarding christianity, based as they are on her ardent attraction to the Roman Catholic faith. It is here that she also debates the role of poet, one that, as we shall see, she renders desirable but problematic, a tension that held consequences for the composition of her own verse.

THE DURHAM YEARS

'Dorothy' Greenwell was born on 6 December 1821, at Greenwell Ford near Lanchester in Durham, to William Thomas Greenwell and Dorothy (née) Smales. Greenwell's father, a country squire and magistrate, was notoriously bad with money and indeed bankrupted the family in 1848. Her mother,

Greenwell's biographers agree, was stern, imperious, self-willed and austere, smothering her daughter into her fiftieth year and, arguably, holding her back, not only from literary fame, but also from intellectual development. It took five years after her mother's death for Greenwell to even comment on this predicament, and even then it was in the coded form of her poem 'Demeter and Cora' (1876). A dialogue between the famous mother and daughter pair, the poem underlines Cora's fear that she is imprisoned by her role: 'still the bars/ Are round me, and the girdling night/ Hath passed within my soul! the stars/ Have risen on me, but the light/ Hath gone for ever' (ll. 18–22). Nevertheless, Greenwell made the most of living at the Ford, producing her first collection of verse here, *Poems* (1848), which itself attests to the fierce dedication Greenwell had to reading. We will return to this point when discussing Greenwell's use of epigraphs, but for now it is enough to say that her earliest influences included the Bible, George Herbert and Mark Akenside, the poetics of which were each vividly marked by a sense of religious beauty. Her Scottish governess introduced Greenwell to eighteenth-century Scottish philosophy, particularly David Hume, and also increased her interest in literature outside England, Greenwell learning German, French, Greek and Latin.[10] She also befriended Josephine Grey (later Butler) around this time, dedicating *The Patience of Hope* (1862) to her and undertaking educative and charitable parish work by her side. Butler's effect on Greenwell was to enhance the poet's predilection for social causes, but her deep religious sense overwhelmed her thoughts and writing from an early age, instilled further by the family's move to live with, first, her eldest brother, William, and, second, her favourite brother, Alan. Both were clergymen. William provided a home for Greenwell and her family at Ovingham Rectory in Northumberland, from where he moved only later to become Canon of Durham. In 1850, the family uprooted themselves once again to Golbourne Rectory in Lancashire, where Alan, a High Church ritualist, held a living. On the death of Greenwell's father in 1854, she and her mother relocated to the religious centre of Durham, where she stayed until 1872, and which provided her with the backdrop against which she produced the majority of her written works.

The reader should not underestimate the consequence of what Greenwell's acquaintance and biographer, William Dorling, called 'The Durham Period'. For Greenwell, Durham proved to be a religious and intellectual mecca of which she was reminded daily, her rooms in the Bailey overlooking the cathedral. Like Barrett Browning, Greenwell was somewhat invalided throughout her adult life, as well as being emotionally overpowered by her mother, and yet she managed to escape these restraints by writing poetry and essays and a significant number of letters. During this time Greenwell exchanged letters with Barrett Browning, Jean Ingelow, Christina Rossetti, William Bell Scott, Thomas Guthrie, William Hanna, William Knight and Thomas Constable. The Constables were Greenwell's main source of cultural activity, Thomas being the son of the eminent Archibald Constable who had published Walter Scott and supervised a number of journals including the *Scots Magazine* and *Edinburgh Review*. Maynard even suggests in her conjecture regarding Greenwell's refusal to marry that 'the real romance' of her life was with the whole Constable family, to whom she began writing in 1859. The reader has only to turn to Greenwell's daring dramatic monologue, 'Christina' (1861), to witness the poet's willingness to rethink the family unit in radical ways. The narrator, a fallen woman, painfully broods upon her relationship with the dying Christina, both 'girlish friends,/ With hearts that, like the summer's half-oped buds,/ Grew close' (ll. 92–4). When the latter passes away, there is some suggestion, although never the realization, that the narrator might become a surrogate daughter, forging what Leighton has called 'a substitutive relationship which radically confuses holy and unholy families'.[11] Greenwell certainly found the Constables as liberating as the narrator of 'Christina' finds her middle-class playmate, and in 1860 she visited them in Edinburgh, their home a consolatory intellectual haven. 'What a boon it is for our hearts and souls to breathe habitually a *climate* such as that of this house,' she wrote, 'where everything good and lovely and to be desired seems not only possible, but natural, and the thing that is nearest to hand: "it makes the Bible easier reading," to quote a saying I heard not long ago of a poor half-witted girl, who, asked if the Bible was the same always, [answered] it was so much easier to read in some houses than others.'[12]

Immersed in the society of the Scottish cultural capital, Greenwell was introduced to William Guthrie, with whom she held a famed conversation on Scottish theology; as one observer noted: 'Miss Greenwell asked questions and the Doctor answered, explained and illustrated. I don't know who most excelled, the answerer or the questioner'.[13] The observer was J. L. Watson, who would later involve Greenwell in the Royal Albert Asylum for Idiots and Imbeciles of the Northern Counties, located in Lancaster. Watson asked Greenwell to edit a series of stories to be sold in order to fund the society and contributors included George Macdonald and Caroline Bowles-Southey.[14] The project also spurred Greenwell to pen 'On the Education of the Imbecile' for the 1868 *Northern British Review*, which, coupled with her other celebrated social paper printed in the same journal six years earlier, 'On Single Women' (1862), and a later paper on the East African Slave Trade for the *Contemporary Review* (1873), established her concerned social voice. Later poems also attest to her interest in welfare, 'The Broken Chain' (1861), for example, imploring the reader to understand the plight of the captive slave, imprisoned and bound not simply by physical constraints, but also by the greater injustice of cultural disapproval.

Greenwell's essays, however, are more direct than her poems, 'On the Education of the Imbecile', marked as it is by the sway of Josephine Butler, and constituting an immediate appeal for better education among what Greenwell labelled the intellectually challenged. 'On Single Women' is equally forthright, being a radical assessment of those women who refrained from partaking of the cultural norm of marriage. 'A single woman!' Greenwell cries, 'Is there not something plaintive in the two words standing together?'[15] 'Single life', she admits, is already 'full of limitations, restrictions', without the fact that the 'traditions of social life are against' such a status, whereon she launches into an attack on the lack of professional training to which women have access.[16] Praising the Society for Promoting the Employment of Women, Greenwell still bemoans the weak role women play in the public sphere, even though 'Woman, whether single or married, is linked with society at every turn, directly or obliquely; her action upon it is increasing'. Professing, then, that women are

54

inseparable from the social fabric, even though they are assumed to be more familiar with the private, domestic space, Greenwell closes by elevating the notion of female independence, noting that 'Woman has already done much for herself *by herself*.[17] This conclusion balances some of the essay's more problematic middle passages, in which Greenwell suggests that in 'imaginative strength' woman 'has been proved deficient', and yet even this is qualified by her deference to the French Catholic, François Fénelon, in his assumption that woman 'is the *soul* of the house, and not its architect'. While a contemporary reader may balk at such an assumption, Greenwell understood Fénelon's comment as in line with her own sense that woman's 'influence in the world is an elemental one, so subtle is it, so continuous, so unperceived'.[18]

Greenwell intimates here that the female imagination, in her view, is spiritual and liquid, able to flow through the world and pick up on the less obvious aspects of its make up. Twentieth-century French feminism would later develop such an idea into a politics, and Greenwell too regards the female mind as somehow more sensuous, subtle and therefore open to ideas that might seem contradictory when regarded in a more straightforward manner.[19] This means that she read the world in a way that enabled her to hold opinions that to others seemed confusing, and nowhere was this more apparent than in her radical understanding of religion.

RELIGION

Greenwell's beliefs, like Hemans's, cannot be addressed through a simple statement of ecclesiastical affiliation, her faith being multi-layered and open to ideas from many theological systems. Aware of the varying christian denominations, she was also captured by other religions, as conveyed in her poem on the Hindu Cupid, 'Madana' (1861), contemplation on the *Mahabharata*, 'The Death of "The Pandavas, or the Five Pious Heroes" ' (1876), and address to the Persian poet, Ferdusi, 'The Song of Islâm' (1876).[20] Like her later poetry, Greenwell's faith was 'experimental' and somewhat baffling to those around her. As Thomas Constable told Dorling, 'she believed so thoroughly in the Catholic Church' and yet 'her personal sympathies were, I think, with Evangelicals and Dissenters'.[21] Constable also recalled, somewhat cheekily, that, on going to church, Greenwell had once told him, ' "I know some go to praise God, and to confess their sins" but "really I own *I go for what I can get*" '.[22] For a more serious assessment of Greenwell's faith, however, we can turn to a quotation from her Evangelical companion and admirer Elizabeth McChesney, which throws much light on the matter:

> The faith of my friend seemed to be always changing in certain directions, and it was very bewildering. She loved the Quakers very much, and the Methodists even better because they are such a strongly social community, and always as she used to say 'liked going to heaven in parties'; and yet in a kind of way she loved all the main doctrines of Rome, and would sometimes talk as though she belonged there. Her brother Alan was at that time a clergyman of an exceedingly High Church type, and she tried to think she was one with him in all things. Curiously enough I never knew her make friends with a High Church or Roman Catholic person, and yet she often spoke as if the Church of Rome embodied typical Christianity, and we Protestants were some kind of aberration from type, necessary, doubtless, but not exactly to be admired.[23]

If we are to follow McChesney, we might work from the assumption that Greenwell found the deepest spiritual consolation in Roman Catholicism, not only because of its dogma, but because of what she perceived to be failures in other belief-systems. Truly, Greenwell considered the 'high' Protestants, or Anglicans, to be in a state of tremendous disarray; while the Ritualists, guilty already for stealing her favourite brother from her, represented a kind of elitist 'class-arrogance' that seemed to play at Romanism without committing to its values.[24]

On the other hand, Low Church Protestantism she found crude and vulgar, and she indirectly addressed such problems in her essay 'Popular Religious Literature' (1866). Here, the reader is confronted with the phenomenon of the ever-swelling market for common treatises on 'homely' devotion, easily surpassed in terms of aesthetic quality, but nevertheless expressive of a kind of holy 'true pathos' that was increasingly in demand.[25] This 'wide, yet barren region' of literature,

Greenwell admits, has 'its lowly, its enduring triumphs', and yet comprises only 'well-intentioned' tracts that have 'no centre, no sequence, no principle of natural cohesion'.[26] Commonly, she argues, the document will read as nothing more than a confusing and 'feverish dream, a complication of never-ending stairs and galleries that lead to nothing'.[27] Communicating only 'some religious truth, or some point of cottage economy' – a dig at Hannah More, perhaps – popular tracts are deemed immodest here because they deliberate about God in a direct fashion.[28] Schiller, she reminds us, dictates 'that a direct object in writing is fatal to a work of high imagination', a contention that applies tenfold to the word of God, inherently a mysterious and unknowable discourse beyond human comprehension.[29] Elementary pamphlets on the subject simply fall short intellectually, not only because moral and devotional issues are neglected, but also because 'their language, in speaking of the Almighty, is not the language of affection, rather that of servility'.[30] This takes us back to Hemans's elevation of affection but, by the time Greenwell was writing, the definition of affection had become so muddied with overtones of excessive sentiment that in *A Present Heaven* affections are dismissed as that which serves to alienate believers from 'the exertion of the intellect'.[31]

Greenwell struggled to reconcile the intellect with the emotions not simply because she was unable to achieve the kind of fusion of feeling and thought Hemans so successfully accomplished, but because she associated the two with apparently diverse religious values. She wrote to William Knight in 1865 that Catholicism she approached '*with the head*, I mean, for with the heart I am altogether Protestant. However much, either in reading or discussion, I may appreciate the value of some great Catholic idea, [when] I kneel down to pray I am Protestant'.[32] The intellect certainly dominated her writings advocating Roman Catholicism, comprising as they do a highly unusual series of perceptions for an ostensibly Protestant thinker. These texts may be divided into two groups. The first consists of Greenwell's direct discussions of Roman Catholicism, and includes her correspondence with William Knight, and her paper 'Is Romanism a Corruption of Christianity, or is it its Natural Development?' (1872). The second set comments more loosely on Catholicism through the idea of the super-natural, a source of spiritual fulfilment that Greenwell promo-ted in her essay 'Prayer', included in *Essays* (1866); and three further papers printed in *Liber Humanitatis* (1875): 'On the Connection between the Animal and Spiritual Nature in Man'; 'On the Relation between Natural and Supernatural Life'; and 'Folk-lore'.[33] Let us begin with Greenwell's letters to Knight, which are reproduced in Dorling's biography and reveal an extensive and profound link between the two writers.

William Knight was Professor of Moral Philosophy at the University of St Andrews and a minister of the Church of Scotland. His own work was abundant, evincing his authori-tative grasp of theology, continental thought and the Words-worths.[34] He had written to Greenwell in 1863, praising her religious commentary *Two Friends*, and met her in Durham some time during the late 1860s. Their correspondence lasted for seven years and provides us with a remarkable record of Greenwell's philosophical, theological and literary knowledge. The most revealing letter Greenwell wrote to Knight regarding her opinions of Roman Catholicism appeared in 1865. It begins with an anxious reference to her biography of Jean-Baptiste-Henri Dominique Lacordaire, an early nineteenth-century Dominican who had revolutionized pulpit oratory through his notoriously emotive sermons. Greenwell was unsure whether to send *Lacordaire* 'for the Press' at this point (she published the biography in 1867), due to Lacordaire's 'Papist' leanings.[35] She wrote: 'I feel as if Catholicism might be disentangled from Popery, and that it probably, in the Providence of God, will yet be so to some effectual degree in great countries, like France or Italy; and that this will be the work of powerful, sincere, and *trained* thinkers'.[36] Encouraging the formation of a kind of Coleridgean clerisy who would reconstruct the Catholic Church, Greenwell intimates, in this first of her written expositions of Rome, that its only oversight is allegiance to the Pope. 'There is nothing in Catholicism, as such, I mean in its doctrines,' she declares, 'that necessarily connects it with the Papacy. Looking at the question historically, I can never see where or when the Pope comes in; after a time you find him there, and can trace how the thing grew, but I never can see that the highest High Church view of the constitution of the

Christian Church as left by the Apostles, with its ordinary government by Bishops, and extraordinary appeal to councils, have any room for one dominant head.'[37]

In constructing her religious identity through her letters to Knight, Greenwell argues that she believes Catholicism to be doctrinally correct, but fears it is institutionally misguided, and publicly expands on such a contention in the 'Romanism' essay. Here she asserts that christianity can be preserved only through recognizing it as an 'imperishable tradition, carried on from age to age; its true "succession" of inspired apostles, its army of elect and martyr spirits' continuing the good fight.[38] Her support for the Catholic idea of Apostolic succession leads her into a more specific defence of 'the Church of Rome', which, if corrupt at all, is so because of 'human agencies' (presumably the Pope) and not its spiritual claims.[39] Moreover, to impugn Catholicism is to denounce Protestantism, she rationalizes, for there is no real difference between the two: 'As to the things most commonly received among us as believers – such as the natural sinfulness of man, his need of supernatural aid', his 'fall in Adam, his spiritual recovery in Christ – there is no point essentially at issue between Catholic and Protestant', she states.[40]

Why then, as McChesney tells us, did Greenwell prefer Catholicism? Greenwell responds to such a query by insisting that 'Roman Catholicism, is the most *evangelical* of all existing communions, because it is the most intense expression of Redemption, and gives the substance of things not seen by an unspiritual world, by, as it were, incarnating the supernatural verities'.[41] By 'evangelical' Greenwell means supernatural, an idea which is pivotal to giving us access to the kind of religion she professed. In Catholic theology, the supernatural implies a going beyond nature into a realm of incorporeal forces and energies and is experienced by mortals through 'grace'. Grace is an internal quality within Catholicism, reached through prayer and which enables us to do 'good' things deserving of salvation. Before the Fall, human nature was already graceful and so supernatural, beyond ignorance, passion, suffering and death, and so offered access to a state of higher perfection that only the angels currently possess. For thinkers like Schiller, the fall of humankind was fortunate, because it allowed us to become more than creatures of instinct, and find a different kind of freedom based on our own moral decisions and choices. Admittedly a risky metamorphosis, humanity's new-found moral nature pushes it into the position where the lost state is continually sought for 'by means of a higher art' that for the Romantics, like Greenwell, has a religious, if not dogmatic, tone.[42] Her desire to 'incarnate' – reflect upon and make real to people – supernatural verities prefigures later nineteenth-century studies like Walter Richard Cassel's *Supernatural Religion* (1874), the last line of which expounds: 'Do not waste life clinging to ecclesiastical dogmas which represent no eternal verities, but search elsewhere for truth which may haply be found'.[43] This elsewhere, or beyond, is not somewhere the subject can reach as if it were a holy grail; instead, for Greenwell, influenced as she is by Schiller, elsewhere accords with one's very being within, our 'living whole', as she writes in 'Prayer'.[44] As M. H. Abrams discerns: 'The result of this way of thinking is to locate the goal of the journey of life in the experience of the journey itself', a statement that directly reflects on Schiller's 'In the eyes of a Reason which knows no limits, the Direction is at once the Destination, and the Way is completed from the moment it is trodden'.[45]

SCHILLER

For Greenwell, like Hemans, Schiller's thought was liberating in its sensitive approach to religious feeling, and she found his philosophy especially perceptive in its impulse to unite the supernatural with reason and rationality: for God, she believed, would never endow spiritual insights on a non-rational being unable to begin to comprehend their weight. In 'Prayer' Greenwell emphasized that christianity is 'a supernatural system based upon a series of supernatural transactions. It is a solemn-world-appealing *fact* – a fact existing along with many other facts', but 'facts of a supernatural order'.[46] One accesses this through the 'supernatural intercourse' of prayer, which must be delivered to God in a state of surrender.[47] The most effective kind of prayer Greenwell called 'slain', indicating that whatever the believer is praying for accords with his or her will which, 'through submission, has become *one* with the will of God'.[48] This fusion of wills creates a moment in which 'spirit acts' 'upon spirit', fulfilling humankind's inherent craving for what she calls elsewhere a 'supersensual' intercourse with whatever lies in excess of what we can materially experience and see.[49] The 'supersensual' thus allows the believer direct access to the 'unseen' spiritual world. In addition, the word signifies a heightened state of reception to God in which the believer might abjectly pray, and one of Greenwell's favourite quotations derived from a friend of Coleridge's who had reported the poet's own supersensual relation to prayer. ' "The most arduous act of the reason and of the will" ', Coleridge professedly declared, is to ' "pray with all your heart and strength, *with the reason and with the will* [. . .] Teach us to pray, oh Lord!" Here he burst into a flood of tears and begged me to pray for him'.[50]

Yet the notion of being 'supersensual' was borrowed not from Coleridge, but from his mentor, Schiller, and notably from the essay 'On Simple and Sentimental Poetry' that would have such a significant impact on Greenwell's later essay, 'An Inquiry: As to how far the spirit of poetry is alien, and how far friendly, to that of Christianity' (1875), to which we will return shortly. At this point, however, it is important to establish why Schiller, and his notion of the supersensual, was so vivid for Greenwell. He was, of course, no Catholic, coming from a Lutheran background and attacking conventional religion as stifling to the soul, and yet Schiller's privileging of what he called 'the religious sense coupled with the spirit of philosophic contemplation' proved consistent with Greenwell's understanding of Catholicism.[51] Schiller arrives at this fusion of divine feeling and rational thought after a prolonged consideration of the differences between 'simple' and 'sentimental' poetry. The first kind of verse, excelled at mainly by the Greeks, owns the power of 'childlike' innocence, describing the object of its composition in a limited, but faithful, manner.[52] 'Sentimental' poetry, however, belongs to the 'moderns', and, unlike simple poetry, imaginatively *'reflects* on the impression produced on' the poet 'by objects'.[53] Only the second type of verse has the capacity to express 'the harmony of feeling and thought' together, thus achieving what Greenwell, like Hemans, wanted religious faith to accomplish.[54] For Schiller, the worst poets are culpable of both the act of flaunting coarse pathos in their work, and the error of addressing sensuous subjects, misdeeds of which he finds Goethe guilty, as Greenwell does in her essay 'The Spirit of Poetry'.[55] Sentimental poets, on the other hand, are able to combine ideas with emotion by treating subjects of the 'supersensuous' order only, 'supersensuous themes' being easily raised to a state of 'spiritual intuition', as opposed to monolithic, didactic poetry.[56] So, too, does the heart of the sentimental poet prefer 'to follow the direction of a lofty spiritual melancholy' that comes close to Greenwell's description of the profoundly emotive experience of prayer, one in which the believer acquiesces to God only to be received into a supernatural realm wherein true faith might develop and endure. Moreover, the supersensual and the supernatural unite in prayer, the first describing the quiet yet passionate words the believer utters, and the second intimating the inexplicable process of transmission by which God receives the appeal.

Greenwell expands on the manner by which this process enables the believer to reach God in 'On the Connection between the Animal and the Spiritual Nature in Man', written after an essay by Schiller of the same title, and addressing the relation between the body and the spirit. Schiller begins his paper by questioning the two theories of the body that governed philosophy in the late nineteenth century: the body, he claims, was deemed either the 'prison-house of the spirit', or, alternatively, the culmination of one's internal thoughts. Both conceptions are misguided, the argument goes, the body and spirit being instead united within the human as one vital force.[57] Accordingly, the senses produce ideas and drive action, the 'operations of thinking and sensation alike' corresponding to what Schiller called the 'internal sensorium', a kind of biologically conceived soul.[58] This soul, however, is ultimately controlled by the 'animal sensations', namely our feelings and passions, which overrule 'the loftiest virtue', the 'profoundest philosophy' and 'even divine religion'.[59] Extremes of emotion, like the 'ecstasy' that issues from intemperate joy, for example, can even disable the whole being of the human, convulsing the brain and its thoughts and able to destroy the 'whole nervous system' that the body is reliant upon.[60] This might all seem very gloomy for a writer like Greenwell, who concurs with Schiller in her acknowledgement that 'unrestrained abandonment' is destined to pass 'into pain'.[61] Yet, for her, the endurance of such pain is an almost bracing factor within faith, testing the believer, who will come out all right if he or she remains true to God. Later in his essay, Schiller foretells this notion in a section on the 'Limitations' of his own theories, wherein he admits that 'a mind courageous and elevated by religion' is 'capable of completely weakening the influence of the animal sensations which assault the soul of one in pain'. The very 'thought of God', interwoven as it is with the universe, can 'spread a bright light' to 'resolve the sensations' of the individual's 'dissolving frame into happiness'.[62] One must feel crushed by the world, it seems, to benefit from the elevating hand of God. If the journey to the spiritual realm is of necessity a painful one, it is here that the supersensual comes back into play, raising the pitch of the feelings the believer must undergo – good and bad – to prepare him or her for the afterworld. As Greenwell suggests, quoting Burns, 'It hardens a' within/ And petrifies the feelin'.'[63]

The believer's success in reaching God, then, is based on faith and Greenwell's was such that she felt unconcerned about the creeping intrusion of secular thought into her society. Like Carlyle, in his proclamation that men cannot do for very long without the devil, she considered it impossible for humanity to function free of God. In 'On the Relation between Natural and Supernatural Life', for example, Greenwell declares: 'Man can do without many things, but there are two which [. . .] he will certainly not forego [. . .] the hope of a future life' and 'the realisation of a present eternal God'.[64] Humanity might be perplexed by the seeming impossibility of the divine, but it will never 'long accept a theory of the universe, with God and with the soul left out'.[65] The reasoning behind this, Greenwell argues, is the presence of, and belief in, the supernatural, invoked more explicitly by Roman Catholicism than Protestantism. For while Protestantism desperately 'seeks its Lord', it wastes time gathering the search party while 'Catholicism is already proclaiming Him'.[66] If, as Greenwell had intimated to

Knight, Protestantism was emotional and Catholicism intellectual, then she sought to elevate the religion she considered most able to deal with the supernatural. For Protestantism, Greenwell mused, contorted the believer's supernatural relationship to God into a gothic performance, and made doctrine sound like folklore. Such a religion cannot help but be 'haunted still "By woman wailing for her demon lover" ', Greenwell wrote, citing Coleridge's 'Kubla Kahn' (1816): Jerusalem viewed through a Protestant lens blurs into Xanadu.[67] The gender implications of such statements are also clear, Catholicism apparently being rational, righteous and thus 'masculine', while Protestantism is compared to the wailing of a woman who easily lends herself to 'that which is oracular and magical'.[68]

If the feminine nature is instinctive and more sensual, this also means, in Greenwell's theological system, that it is allied 'to the spiritual' rather than the supernatural.[69] Such a binary is taken to the extreme in Greenwell's *Two Friends*, in which the narrator recalls her conversations with 'Philip', a fictional clergyman, who, though presumably Protestant, holds some rather Roman Catholic beliefs. This male voice, Greenwell told Knight in a letter of 1868, was 'meant to represent [my] practical working side, which in fact is a much more strong and real part of my mind than the imaginative'.[70] Only 'Philip', rather than the unnamed female narrator, can recognize that Protestantism fails to engage the supernatural because it gets stuck in the spiritual, lacking that which is needed to elevate the believer into the supernatural and then into heaven. Moreover, this very arrest is due to its 'strange jealousy of the supernatural' which bars it from '*grace*; the voice of the Divine Spirit wakening up the human spirit to its true life'.[71] This argument is profoundly Catholic: grace, acquired through prayer, is a 'supernatural gift' that both habitually and actually brings one closer to God: only a male narrator, it seems, can voice such a strongly Roman doctrine.

POETRY AND RELIGION

Two Friends is an important book because it introduces Greenwell's first pronounced difficulties with the relationship

64

between poetry and religion, the question with which this chapter opened. Early in the dialogue, 'Philip' seems to suggest there is no tension to worry about: 'I have long loved art and poetry, because I saw that they had a power to raise and soften Humanity; more lately I have seen that *they are good in themselves*'.[72] He accuses the narrator of being both afraid of 'the broad, free sweep of imaginative greatness, as being in some way antagonistic to the spirit of Christ', and in dread of 'the free development of art'.[73] She agrees, seeing in art and literature 'the absorbing, intoxicating devotion they demand, something which reminds me of the Greek worship of Dionysius'.[74] The antagonism between art and religion is brought sharply into focus, however, by Philip's submission to the narrator's view, put forth in a passage that sets his reading of Keats against his parish duties:

> I shall never forget sitting at an open window of a little parsonage, in the west of England, during great part of a golden summer's afternoon, reading Keats; the garden was full of flowers, and I read my book to the scent of the mignonette and pinks, as to a music stealing within every sense. It was one of those warm, brooding days that steep the spirit in delight; all around was silence, the stillness, not so much of sleep as of nature in a blissful dream. Then an uneasy consciousness came across me, breaking the delicious spell. I ought to be setting forth on my parish round. I started. First on my list came an aged woman, almost stone-deaf, ignorant, but anxious. I had to sit beside her before a huge fire; her son worked at his loom in an inner room, and did not cease when I began to read. How hot and noisy the cottage seemed; how contracted all around me! Had the world of light and beauty I lived and moved in but half an hour ago *collapsed* into this? How confused, too, seemed my own statements, my very utterance thick and hesitating, as of one under a heavy thrall, for my heart was with Endymion, and I had to tell the story of Christ.[75]

The two scenes evoked are stark opposites: Philip languishes amidst his Keatsian fantasies, intoxicated by the stillness of the natural world as he is lulled by the musical power of poetry. His parish obligations are anathema to such a world, however, intruding upon the quiet repose of his poetical bower and forcing him to confront the alternate extremes of social life among the poor. It is with 'uneasy consciousness' that Philip sets out on his rounds and he remains within this state of blunted confusion even while declaiming the gospel, anaesthetised to the passionate sufferings of Christ by the beauty of *Endymion* (1818).

The tension between poetry and religion is unresolved in *Two Friends*, and it was only later, in 'The Spirit of Poetry', that Greenwell addressed the subject again in some detail. In the intervening fifteen or so years, Greenwell would read, and quote, almost obsessively from both religious and secular writers, mainly English, German and French and often poets. As briefly noted earlier, her fixation on citing short passages by other writers took the art of using epigraphs to the extreme, granting her work a certain depth and evincing to her readers her intellectual endeavours. *A Basket of Summer Fruit* (1877), for example, is so crammed with quotations from all manner of writers that it is hard to recognize it as a set of eight essays on faith, critics often mistaking it for an anthology. Works by Coleridge, Wordsworth, Schiller and Barrett Browning are most often cited, Goethe, Kant, George Herbert and Frederick William Faber coming close behind. Whether it be Chaucer, Elizabeth I, Spenser, Milton, Susanna Wesley, Akenside, Byron, Thoreau, Tennyson, Clough, Michelet, Newman, Pusey or Shelley in the epigraphical dock, Greenwell generally chose excerpts from their writing that fed into her discussion of the relationship between religion and poetry. For example, her first collection of poetry is introduced with a quotation from Akenside's *The Pleasures of the Imagination* (1757):

> Beauty, sent from Heaven
> The lovely ministress of Truth and Good
> In this dark World; for Truth and Good are one,
> And Beauty dwells with them, and they in her
> With like participation.

(Book I, ll. 432–6)

Immediately the debate is staged: beauty, or aesthetics, must be relayed from heaven because of its inherent implication of truth and goodness, ideas fresh to Greenwell from Kant's *The Critique of Judgement* (1790). Elsewhere, she is fascinated by Kant's advocation in this study of words like 'I *can* and I *ought* – words in which we may say the whole science of morals is wrapped up – words in which the ideals of duty, freedom and personal accountability lie enfolded – "Infinite riches in a little room" '.[76] The moral implications of aesthetics is an unwieldy field of discussion that Greenwell enters into only tentatively, and always in terms of its connection to religious faith. Moral inquiry itself detracts from one's focus on religion, the poet argued in *A Basket of Summer Fruit*, citing Barrett Browning's indictment of 'morals' as that which leads the believer 'to entertain/ Impossible plans of superhuman life'.[77] More important is to experience religion emotionally, as one gathers from Greenwell's championing of Roman Catholicism, and yet this sets up another dilemma: is too much feeling, like too much poetry, a distraction from the christian path?

The extent of this dilemma is vividly apparent in Greenwell's often contradictory thoughts on the subject. In a letter to William Knight from 1866, for example, she attacks the notion of christianity as solely creed or conviction, but also worries that its ability to affect the individual sentimentally is the 'cause to which we may trace much of which its adversaries have had reason to reproach it with'.[78] Shelley, for example – one of Greenwell's favourite poets and an unlikely admirer of Hemans – famously deemed christianity 'the "most awful of all religions" ' because of its fanatical enthusiasm, compelling Greenwell to rely instead on Wordsworth's stoical belief-system in which one lives a christian life through 'mental and moral diet, and *regimen*'.[79] She was fond of those celebrated lines in Wordsworth's 'The Tables Turned': 'One impulse from a vernal wood/ May teach you more of man/ Of moral evil and of good/ Than all the sages can', which she cited in her essay 'On the Dignity of the Human Body'.[80] But again, the grandeur of nature, which was still fuelling the pantheist movement through the nineteenth century, was at once inspirational and beguiling, forcing Greenwell back upon thinkers like Madame Guyon, who argued that God's authentic blessing could only be received after the believer agreed to conform entirely with the divine will.[81] Yet, returning to her beloved Shelley, along with Byron and Burns, Greenwell perceived how their verse represented the mighty power imagination and 'ardent feeling' owned to 'let in heaven upon the soul, and flood it with the warmth and radiance' of the poet's dreams.[82]

Such dreams were also perilous, however, and Greenwell used a quotation from 'Kubla Kahn' to declare that even her Catholic hero Lacordaire observed a religious track which 'from time to time' sank 'suddenly into darkness and silence, as if to run through subterranean depths, "And caverns, measureless to man,/ Down to a sunless sea" '.[83]

Greenwell's back-and-forth attitude towards the role of feeling and poetry is laid out in a more controlled manner in 'The Spirit of Poetry', beginning from the teasing premise that the two might be concordant. 'At first sight', Greenwell suggests, 'poetry would seem the natural ally of Christianity. Poetry, like Christianity, gives wings to the fettered soul [and] like Christianity, poetry speaks to man of something that is far beyond.' Equally, both 'betray a noble discontent with the things that do appear', each grappling with a material world that provides little fulfilment for the individual soul.[84] Further more, christian and poet alike are commensurate targets of persecution for excusing themselves from 'time and circum-stance', the worldliness of existence unattractive to each.[85] Just as poetry has the only true power to render God accessible to mortal minds, so God's word is poetical, Greenwell insisting that there is 'no grander poem than the Book of Job'.[86]

Yet the way in which poetry and religion versically treat their subject matter is where the consonance between them starts to crumble. Nature, for instance, dominant in verse since pastoral, Greenwell reminds us, is a theme poetry seeks to 'exalt and intensify' and make a kind of springboard from which it might reach 'further than nature itself in its leading upon dangerous, forbidden paths'.[87] Poetry is 'the soul's intoxication, its illusion', urging 'onward the passions which nature herself would seek to hold in leash' and finding 'food for a "darker ecstasy" '.[88] Christianity, however, Greenwell argues, desires to 'depress' nature, Christ 'at war' with it in his role as 'the pruner, the purifier', purging the 'vine' of its opiate fruit while poetry encourages the untamed budding of 'many clustered' 'wild grapes'.[89] As the poet allows 'over-strained emotion' to dictate his or her wandering course, the christian's aim 'is single "Before him is an ever-fixed mark;/ He looks on tempests and is never shaken" ', although there is something ironic in Greenwell's use of a Shakespearean line of poetry to indicate religion's difference from verse.[90] Yet she remains determined that religion 'lives to order and to law; its object is to repress nature, to suppress passion', while poetry 'can only exist in an atmosphere of emotion, which, if it fails to find, it will go out of its way to create'.[91]

Poetry, then, seems rather excessive against christianity's discipline, although sometimes, Greenwell admits, it is this which helps believers in their pursuit of the divine. For in the lyric, poetry's 'most intense form', the believer has access to 'some rare moment' within 'a world of feeling' that deems the poet, 'if no prophet', at least 'a seer', his or her 'eye, gifted with the vision and the faculty divine' to pierce 'deeper into the heart of things' than most.[92] This advantage, however, is one to which poetry sometimes falls prey: Greenwell's model here is Goethe's *Faust* (1808/1832), wherein 'we see all that which in life is beautiful, tender and nobly aspiring, wrecked against all that which is base'.[93] Such sentiments echo her earlier warning to Knight in a letter from 1868, wherein she claims of the drama, 'What an awful book it is! Its greatness I feel', yet does 'it not prove morally that Goethe delights in things as they are? and how little lovely, or even great, is his idea of God! A mere Artificer on a grand scale! There is no true, no moral greatness.'[94] The problem with *Faust* here is that it represents the inherently 'mutinous spirit' of poetry, a phrase used by William Michael Rossetti to describe poetry's disposition to 'arraign God himself'.[95]

The notion of poetry as a rebellious force striking against the divine is dangerous, argues Greenwell, because of its capacity to inflect verse of all forms, religious and secular alike. Not only does poetry's insurgent character illuminate 'regions where we might expect it', in the work of 'men like Byron, and like Burns', but also in that of 'men of a calmer, more philosophical temperament, such as were some of the great Elizabethan dramatists' and 'the old troubadours'.[96] Yet, for her, the perhaps unexpected reason why poetry has such seditious force is that it owns a harsher nature than even christianity, 'whether in its bitter and vindictive, or in its tender and plaintive mood', driving 'in the dart of anguish still deeper' where the latter consoles, even when austere.[97] Poetry dictates more than religious discipline, it seems, pushing

69

readers into a state of 'lawlessness' where they must endure a kind of never-ending struggle wherein consolation is always absent.[98] Such a struggle persists in readers because coaxed by the imagination, which, since the Romantics, had been conceived of as a dynamic but unsettling energy. Notably, Greenwell's conception of this idea was most affected by Shelley's notion of the imagination as a lightning rod that strikes the thinker, thus provoking in him or her a powerful epiphanic vision of the world which, for Shelley, necessarily involved a sudden awareness of God's absence. Poetry can consequently only produce 'scepticism' in its reader, planting a deep sense of loss which it always promises to fulfil even though it clearly cannot do so. Both the poet and christian strive to counter such loss, and while it is here that they 'meet, here too they separate, like friends who, coming across each other on the wide ocean or upon some high upland path, embrace, commune together, perhaps only for a moment, and then start upon far-diverging paths'.[99] Each 'ponder[s] deeply over the painful riddle of the earth', but 'while the poet's ardent and irritable feelings are wrung and tortured by the view of outward discord, the Christian's submissive heart is oppressed by the deep alienation caused by inward sin'.[100]

How halting Greenwell's argument seems, then. She wavers between favouring the poet, a figure who enhances the world God has made, to preferring the christian, one better equipped to dealing with the pain intrinsic to society. Her closing comments are no less arresting, as she seems at last to declare the christian champion of all, able at once sparingly to taste the 'intoxicating wild honey' of poetry as well as the profound waters of religious faith. The true christian 'will seldom, I think, quaff a very deep draught from this broad, full river, though he may listen awhile to its murmur as it flows, now half subterraneously, now flashing clearly to the day "From caverns measureless to man,/ Down to a sunless sea" '.[101] This is in itself an impasse, it would seem, Greenwell using Coleridge, primarily acknowledged as a poet, to elevate the figure of the christian. As stated above, Greenwell also implemented these lines from 'Kubla Kahn' to describe her view of Lacordaire's christian progress, and they point to her own view of poetry and religion as it surfaces in her verse. For

Coleridge's poem at least attempts to reconcile the forces of poetry and religion, dream vision and divine reverie, setting up a number of fragile binary oppositions in its exploration of the cosmic paradise of Xanadu. This at once ethereal and palpable world seems now 'romantic', now 'savage', 'sunless' yet 'fertile', 'holy' but 'enchanted'; even its centre point, a 'sunny pleasure dome', is riven with 'caves of ice' (ll. 5, 6, 12, 14, 36). The 'woman wailing for her demon-lover' in line 16 casts a gothic aura over the scene which betrays Kahn's impaired vision and indicates the dangerous power his natural landscape possesses. Like Greenwell, who had used the wailing woman image in 'Folklore' to convey the threat any kind of excess posed to religion, Coleridge dreaded nature's usurpation of God, coming eventually to regard it as 'the devil in a straight waistcoat'.[102] Further, Coleridge's synthesizing attempt to conciliate the contradictions within Kahn's nirvana parallels Greenwell's own desire to dissolve the dissension between poetry and religion. Both seek a type of philosophical unity between the process of 'creating' and 'believing' that enabled them to write poetry, even though in like manner they eventually turned to the essay as their dominant mode of expression.

POETICS

Greenwell's poetry often seems of its time: her verse moves between the established genres of sonnet, hymn, ballad, the extended elegy and dramatic monologue, sometimes reaching for lyrical intensity, while at others seeming content with a more colloquial tone. As Bernard Richards reminds us in his overview of Victorian poetry, since the Renaissance poetical genres had tended to merge and metamorphose, and Greenwell exploited this inclination, especially in her experimental, blank verse.[103] She does not gush, containing her lines in neat stanzaic patterns, but her appeals to intense feeling are nevertheless marked by notes of exclamation that echo the enthusiastic religious poetry of Edward Young and James Thomson. The pastoral element to much of her poetry she owes to the Wordsworths, William and Dorothy alike, and the musically theological tone of Christina Rossetti is ever present, although Greenwell is not nearly as innovative. She may simply have feared that poetry was a lapsed genre, not only because of its distance from religion, but also because, like Hemans, she registered that it was in a period of serious decline. In *Camera Obscura*, for example, she cites a particularly despondent passage from Clough in which he bemoans the fallen status of the god of poetry, Apollo: 'No longer by clear spring or shady grove, no more on any Pindus or Parnassus, or by the side of any Castaly, are the true haunts of the poetic powers; but if we could believe it, if anywhere, in the blank and desolate streets and upon the solitary bridge of the midnight city, where guilt is, and wild temptation, and the dire compulsion of what has once been done there. With these tragic Sisters round him, and with Pity also, walks the discrowned Apollo.'[104]

Only towards the end of the century was the poetry of the 'streets' and the 'midnight city' fully developed, and yet Greenwell's less conventional later verse follows a mode which the modern reader might recognize as stream-of-consciousness. Her earlier verse, by contrast, is stylistically, if not always thematically, conservative and uses similar motifs to those used by Procter and Rossetti. Indeed, she often addressed women writers as the subjects of her verse: the famous 'Christina' was arguably inspired by Rossetti's philanthropic work with fallen women, and 'To Christina Rossetti' reads as a direct address to this poet she so admired. Anne Woodrooffe's novels also spurred two short sonnets, and two further sonnets, returned to below, heralded Greenwell's own poetic connections with Barrett Browning. The dedication of the 1867 *Poems* to the memory of Barrett Browning reasserts Greenwell's identification with her, quoting as it does from Schiller's *Don Carlos* (1787), 'If I despair of being like to thee,/ I, for such likeness, give thee boundless love'. Strong female figures too are everywhere points of contemplation for Greenwell: Madana, the Hindu Cupid (1861); Sita, the divine wife of Rama (1869); Potaminca, Basilide's burned virgin (1876); and the Russian duchess, Maria Ivanovna, all versified upon (1867); while girls, maidens, wives, sisters, brides and daughters are the commonest recipients of her song.[105] She is sometimes evangelical, *Songs of Salvation* offering a number of patronizing conversion poems reeling with religious cliché; and at other times she is erudite, notably in her observations on doctrine, 'Reserve' (1861), 'Quis Separabit?', 'Summa Theologiae' and 'The Cross' (1869) providing profound commentaries on prayer, the gospel, hell and christian love. Greenwell also flirts with originality, 'On Visiting an Artist's Studio' (1848) predating Rossetti's 'In an Artist's Studio' by eight years, and 'The Garden of Proserpine' (1869) echoing the mellifluous harmonies of Swinburne's poetry.[106] Finally, she seems close to symbolism in her fragmentary blank verse, which is intrepidly imagist and occasionally rhythmic, but always strikingly religious. 'A Mystery', 'Desolate, but not Forsaken' and 'Christus et Ecclesia', for example, all included in *The Soul's Legend* (1873), are notable for their effusion of a sense assembled of Protestant faith, Catholic supernaturalism and Chinese mysticism.

To work through Greenwell's development as a poet is to follow the trajectory her own collections evince: her 1848 and 1850 poems play out stock elegiac narratives that will be refined in the 1861 and 1867 collections, and gradually experimented with in her editions of 1869, 1873 and 1876. Greenwell's early poems appeared in two volumes, the popular *Poems* (1848), and its sequel, *Stories that Might be True, with Other Poems* (1850). *Poems* is a typical expression of the aching sentiments that haunted the anxious Victorian poet, mourning, winter, graves, ruins, vigils and memorials all soliloquized upon. 'The Mourning of the Gael', for example, uses a Scottish grieving tradition to invoke the consolatory notion that the dead 'have not left us' as long as 'Our hearts have not yet learned to say farewell!', the 'bright chain of Love' straining but 'not broken' (ll. 16, 18, 27). Similar tensions are respected in 'Winter-Song', Greenwell figuring the icy winter season as a 'noiseless sprite' who silently murders the year, covering its 'corpse' in a 'shroud of snow' (ll. 4–5). Only the 'pure flame of charity' that kindles within the domestic home can melt this glacial sense of death, the bright 'household hearth' uniting with the 'Heart' to 'keep out the chill' (ll. 45, 48, 60).

The solace of family life, perhaps missing in Greenwell's own household, is rarely idealized in these early poems, the anonymity of life a prominent theme. In 'The Silent Grave-Stone', she versifies upon a monument marked simply 'Hugo', discovered while walking through Lillington churchyard in Warwickshire, not far from Leamington Spa where she received treatment from the renowned Dr Henry Jephson in the early 1840s.[107] Very conscious of the fragility of the body at this time as a consequence, Greenwell directs her narrator to muse upon the 'restless energy of common life', soothed only by 'the calm influence of God's quiet field' (ll. 10, 12). Yet she recognizes that such comfort comes at the expense of a 'chastened spirit' that is reliant on the prayers of the still living to ease it into the 'Court of Peace' (ll. 11, 14). Anonymous in the tomb, however, Hugo seems without relief: 'Was there no voice to soothe, no eye to weep,/ No heart, affection's vigil-watch to keep', the narrator apprehensively asks (ll. 32–3). Only Christ, the narrator suggests, can replace parental 'fondess' with a form of spiritual love that goes beyond 'Brother's love' (ll. 67–8). Similarly, in 'The Vigil of Rizpah', a 'lonely watcher' keeps a 'solemn tryst' with her own 'anguish', broken-hearted and in agony as to whether she might trust 'Love's untiring might' (ll. 1–4). Again, it is the 'reconciling tears' of heaven that finally comfort her, alone in the darkness of sleepless nights but God barring all 'savage thing' from the scene to allow her 'holy grief' to culminate and fade (ll. 11–12).

Yet these early poems also demonstrate a concerted effort on the author's part to construct herself as a visionary poet, using religious iconography to assert her at once dreamy and sacred gaze. Two poems that exemplify this are the double sonnet 'On Visiting an Artist's Studio' and the sonnet 'Written in the Blank Leaf of "Proverbial Philosophy"'. Both use the image of a church to initiate a monologue on the connection between religious architecture, decoration and knowledge, the latter communicated most easily, the poems suggest, through bright, ritualistic imagery. Like much Tractarian poetry, which uses interior church adornment to illustrate religious truth to the laity, these verses are touched by a High Church sensibility that Greenwell would have been surrounded by when she wrote them. Moving from her brother's estate to Durham, she uses the narrator of the double sonnet to marvel at the 'ancient pile' of the cathedral as it intimates all that is unseen in the holy world, 'From the bright real to the things that seem' (ll. 22). Compared to the magical realm of the artist's studio, wherein 'ethereal' fantasies are made material on canvas, the church becomes an equally private and enchanted place where the concealed mysteries of God are made apparent (l. 13). This idea is underlined in 'Written in the Blank Leaf', a 'Gothic temple' dominating the scene of the poem from line 1, and the 'symbols' marked on the temple walls, 'shin[ing] of holiest mysteries', confronting the reader in line 3. The beauty of the interior sanctuary described here is portrayed, not only by the 'golden fruitage set in mouldings fair', the 'rich illumined' missals and lavish 'saintly robes that God's high priest did wear', but also by God's truth itself, which 'shines through vermeil-tinctur'd blazonries' (ll. 5–7). Only in such incense-filled haze are 'hidden meanings' spoken to the 'faithful ear'; wisdom, far from seeming esoteric and distanced from those who worship within, is 'serene and clear', as if enthroned, elevated and so clarified by the splendour of its surroundings (ll. 10, 14).

The notion of keeping back religious truth from those unprepared to receive it was called 'reserve' in the High Church, having been affirmed by Tractarianism at the time Alan, Greenwell's brother, was enthralled by the movement.[108] Reserve required that God's scriptural laws should remain hidden to all but the faithful, and urged commentators on theology to encode or restrict their presentation of religious knowledge. Metaphor, figure and allegory of the kind only an initiated believer might understand were thus used to render religious truth within devotional poetry and biblical exegesis alike. It was a popular idea with religious poets, Keble, Isaac Williams, Rossetti and Procter enjoying Tractarianism's privileging of the oblique, psalm-like, reverent overtones of poetry as the most reserved of genres. The doctrine is particularly helpful in examining Greenwell's poetical development because it provides a point of comparison between her 1848 and 1861 poems, being a subject she addresses in both collections within the corralled and so restrained sonnet form.

There are several differences between the earlier 'Written in the Blank Leaf' and the later poem, 'Reserve', however. In the second composition, the language is tighter, more succinct, and

Greenwell often employs the technique of beginning new sentences mid-line to halt the reader into poetical pauses. In the earlier poem, everything crudely 'shines' in the church, God's word embraced by an almost too lavish atmosphere. The later composition, however, deems the reception of sacred knowledge more 'noble' than sensuous, unwinding the 'deeper, rarer harmonies' with a subtle touch (ll. 1, 4). Moreover, the earlier sonnet implies that religious truth, while reserved, should be on offer for those able to interpret its signs, whereas 'Reserve' is more prohibitive: here the 'crowd' must be restrained from these mysteries, while the older, wiser and more linguistically skilled narrator is rendered suitably prepared 'to drink in all thy Being's overflow' (ll. 11, 14).

Greenwell's increased dexterity as a poet is reflected in many of the 1861 and 1867 verses, the enchanting 'Silence', for example, reflecting once again on the significance of adopting a reserved stance before God but in melodious tones she had hitherto not reached.[109] 'I turn unto the Past/ When I have need of comfort', the speaker begins, constructing memories as a source of tranquil consolation, the poem's very narrative a Wordsworthian spot of time (ll. 1–2). Ostensibly, the poem recalls a poetry-reading that is given following a countryside walk; and yet, as the recital commences, the reader is so spellbound by the aura that issues from the poem, that he pauses to immerse himself in a silence that overawes his audience. Greenwell's very poetic diction parallels this by easing her own reader into a moment of repose, as these lines describing the walk convey:

> On the hill
> That noon in summer found us; far below
> We heard the river in a slumbrous flow
> Chide o'er its pebbles, slow and yet more slow;
> Beneath our feet the very grasses slept
> Signed by the sliding sunbeam as it crept
> From blade to blade, slow stealing with a still
> Admonitory gesture.

(ll. 8–15)

The recurrence of the word 'slow' here is immediately disengaging, lulling the reader into a quiescent yet heightened state that prepares him or her for the 'thrill' that suddenly runs 'lightly through the wood' in the succeeding clause: 'me-thought a Spirit's sign/ Had then been audible, but none came by/ To trouble us, and we were silent', the narrator concedes (ll. 15–16, 18–20). His expectation that spirits haunt his environment intensifies further the animated atmosphere that the speaker enters into on reading out loud the group's 'chosen Poet' (l. 22). As the gathering listen, so

> the reader's voice let fall
> Its flow of music; sweet as was the song
> He paused in, conquered by a spell more strong
> We asked him not its cadence to recall.
> It seemed as if a Thought of God did fill
> His World.
>
> (ll. 25–9)

The sublime hush that falls on the narrator and his company becomes representative of the 'Silence' they will find in heaven, and the 'deep poverty' of mortal 'Speech', not so as to condemn poetry, but in order to elevate the significance of musing upon verse (ll. 34, 37–8). Greenwell thus alerts the reader to the power poetry holds to both bring about and liberate contemplation and thought, especially that directed towards God, but also that which she hopes will issue from the study of her own words. For 'Silence' maps out a way of reading that is careful, full of feeling and yet deeply pensive, suggesting that it is in verse that the problems of her age might be worked through and rectified.

This is apparent in the robust poem 'The Nineteenth Century', which opens a section appropriately designated 'Liber Veritatis', the truth being, Greenwell implies, that poetry, the very genre that promises redemption and consolation, is being neglected within her times. The twenty-five-line poem is a remarkable commentary on the demise of poetry, blamed here on a zeitgeist too deeply entrenched in the project of empire, progress and materialism. The nineteenth century, figured as a 'stern and proud' mother figure, is rendered uncaring and absent-minded, listening only for the 'crashing' of poetry's fall and thinking nothing of 'pastoral stop or reed' (ll. 1, 5–6). Her thoughts are instead:

>   vowed
> To tasks of might, and thou thyself wilt be
> Thy Poet, finding in thy stormy tunes
> Rough music.

(ll. 6–9)

'Rough music' is little comfort for the narrator, however, increasingly angered by an era in which 'no Bard' has the will to 'chronicle' the march of progress, that which lacks poetic melody, too uncivil and turbulent for the 'praise of gentle-hearted singers!' (ll. 10–11, 13). Heeding Clough's lament for the death of Apollo, the narrator here fears that only the despotic drive within the period will triumph, softly and yet sneakily declaring its power: 'Thou wilt raise/ The crown to thine own brows, and calmly claim/ The Empire thou hast won' (ll. 13–15). For this is a time that has 'no Name' to 'conjure with', a time that has irresponsibly miscomprehended the strength of its own 'gigantic' steps, unaware of the 'portents vast' that 'Loom round thy path, where good and evil cast' (ll. 19–20). More dismal still is the apparent absence of any poet to challenge such treachery and ignorance: 'as yet no Prophet doth appear/ In all thy sons', the narrator grieves (ll. 22–3). If Greenwell bemoans the lack of inspiration among the period's 'sons' here, however, she appears more than willing to invest in one of its daughters in the same collection, as 'To Elizabeth Barrett Browning, in 1851' and 'To Elizabeth Barrett Browning, in 1861' reveal. While the second sonnet is a fairly customary in memoriam, the first reads like a mystical address to a Christ-figure, the narrator intoxicated and literally over-whelmed by the skill of the older poet: 'My soul, like Sheba's Queen, faints, overcome,/ And all my spirit dies within me, numb,/ Sucked in by thine, a larger star' (ll. 4–6). Like a bee, the narrator becomes drunk on the 'bloom' of Barrett Browning's verse, and yet the latter's linguistic exhibitions own a 'strength' so mighty that the now subdued younger poet is forced to confess: 'I feel as if I ne'er could sing again!' (ll. 9, 13–14).

If this sense of paralysis affected Greenwell at all, it was in the marked transformation of her poetical mode throughout her writing of the 1870s, attesting as it does to a modern, experimental phase in her career. 'Oh, amiable, lovely death!' (1869), for example, is a long, free-verse religious commentary on the path to death, the believer passing through the membrane of the mortal world to reach God: 'For the heavens shall be clear above me, clear to their very depths, without cloud or stain;/ Terrible in their clearness even as the burning sapphire, I shall look up through them to the throne of God' (ll. 47–8). This material world enmeshes the believer, however, tempting him or her with the tangible beauty of nature, 'the passion-flower' that 'carries in her heart the tokens of an eternal torture' and 'the sworded lilies, blood-red, death-pale' that 'flash in the broad light of noon' (ll. 5, 9). Only when this 'summer is over' can the believer begin to throw off the 'pain' that comes from temporal existence, 'though it be lithe and searching as the cold fanged snake' (ll. 32, 40). Such vivid imagery becomes a hallmark of this sinuous, wandering poetry, instilled as it is with a force intent on entering into combat with the vicious power of all that is not heaven. 'Si Descendero in Infernum, Ades', too, uses the earthly image of the ocean to convey hell, rendered as a murky weed-filled realm, trapping its inhabitants with bloodthirsty glee, the vitality of the breaking waves satanically agile. The reader is lured into feeling the physical conflict between the infernal waters and the narrator, the latter exclaiming: 'Weeds, weeds around my heart, that choke and press,/ And drag my spirits downwards unto lands/ Of dire forgetfulness' (ll. 14–16). Further poems such as 'Remembrance', 'A Life-Requiem', 'November' and 'Buried, yet not dead' score the pages of *Carmina Crucis* (1869) with a similarly ominous sense of struggle against worldly pursuits that is rarely broken, exceptions such as the cheerily devotional 'Christ's Garland' out of place in this sombre book.

While Greenwell sometimes pulled away from poetic convention, neglecting the order imposed by rhyme, stanzaic pattern and iambic pentameter, she continued to invest in typical nineteenth-century themes throughout her life. The Arnoldian 'Between Two Worlds' of *Camera Obscura* is a typical example of this, the narrator caught in a purgatorial 'sea of terrible crystal rent/ With fire' and rushed at by a flock of speeding spirits 'locked in long despair, 'twixt Earth and

Heaven' (ll. 1–2, 62). As the spirits clamour to lament their carnal desires, tormented by the seeming discord between their world and the next, the narrator attempts to intervene between the two spheres and reconcile them. Yet, as she speaks, she is forced to admit to a 'weariness/ Of men and things' that 'at my spirit gnawed', a prevailing sense of antagonism between humanity and God haunting her, as it possessed Greenwell throughout her career as a writer (ll. 116–17). The narrator here concludes with a compromise: earth remains 'still and heaven its silence kept', endlessly deferring the problem of how these two wholly different spheres might make sense to the believer caught between the two. Greenwell also deferred the issue, forever analysing the fracture between poetry and religion while persevering with her own writing and practising the christian faith until the end of her life. When her mother died in 1871, Greenwell moved between London and Torquay, until an accident rendered her dependent once again upon Alan, with whom she lived in Clifton from 1881. She died the following year, and was buried in Arno's Vale Cemetery in Bristol, but the popularity of her works endured until the twentieth-century distaste for religious writing set in, deeming her a minor author where it had neglected the lyrical gifts of Hemans.

4

Adelaide Anne Procter

'That child', said Fanny Kemble of the young Adelaide Anne Procter, 'looks like a poet's child, and a poet. It has something "doomed" in its appearance.'[1] Kemble's early memory of Procter anticipates the general public perception of our third poet, Charles Bruce knowingly declaring in 1875 that: 'She well knew what pain meant'.[2] In his Introduction (1866) to her collected verse, however, Charles Dickens highlighted her 'delight in humour', 'cheerfulness' and 'noble heart':

> No claim can be set up for her, thank God, to the possession of any of the conventional poetical qualities; she never by any means held the opinion that she was among the greatest of human beings; she never suspected the existence of a conspiracy on the part of mankind against her; she never recognised in her best friends, her worst enemies; she never cultivated the luxury of being misunderstood and unappreciated; she would far rather have died without seeing a line of her composition in print, than that I should have maundered about her, here as 'The Poet', or 'The Poetess'.[3]

Dickens's refusal to grant her a poet-status he considered indulgent and melancholic has helped to rescue Procter from the kind of endless conjecture around her private life that has confused studies of women like Letitia Landon, and, albeit to a lesser extent, Hemans. Yet he simultaneously extinguished modern interest in a woman who was not only the best-selling poet of the nineteenth century bar Tennyson, but Queen Victoria's favourite poet, her death in 1864 described by the press as a 'national calamity'.[4] Her collected poems, published as *Legends and Lyrics*, was regularly reprinted up to 1913 and her most famous poem, 'A Lost Chord' (1860), was set to music by Sir Arthur Sullivan. A literary Princess Diana, then, Procter captured the crisis of the mid-nineteenth century that Hemans had so accurately anticipated, namely that 'feeling', still best rendered through poetry, would come under attack in a society increasingly suspicious of religious values and emotional output. As Margaret Maison states of Procter: 'She appears to have taken over where Felicia Hemans left off, as the sweetly feminine and refined purveyor of pretty sentiments in verse, the graceful, tender poetess, the mainstay of bijou almanacs, birthday books and musical evenings'.[5] Bewildered by the heavy sentimentalism of much Victorian writing, readers often struggled with their ability to feel in this period and Procter's poetical working-through of the paralysis of articulation and reception offered her huge readership a consolatory philosophy with profound salvific qualities.

Procter's expression of feeling was as powerful and subversive as Hemans's had been, fuelling her poetry on many social issues concerning women and the poor, as well as love and religion, her conversion to Roman Catholicism in 1851 rendering her the most popular Catholic poet of her day. Her poetry fuses a joint loyalty to the political feminism of the Langham Place Group, and to the late Romantic project to communicate feeling, supported by her father and headed by Wordsworth and Hemans. Both Procter's parents would have a profound influence on their literary daughter, born to them in London on 30 October 1825. Bryan Waller Procter, as member of the 'Cockney school', known by his pseudonym, Barry Cornwall, had been attacked and feminized for his premise that poetry must struggle to articulate disturbing emotions. Procter's consistent wrangling with the difficulty of expression, then, deals with the failure of her father's emotive poetry as well as with the wider issue of how all of us might voice that which concerns us most. As her most recent biographer, Gill Gregory, argues, 'it is Procter's concern with the capacity for expression and the problems of articulation, her preoccupation with what lies unexpressed and dormant within ourselves, that accounts for her popularity. She writes of women who struggle for an articulate voice and defined place in the world.'[6] Isobel Armstrong too points to the 'abruptly economical' tone of her lyrics, Procter employing an aesthetic reserve that is curbed in order to effuse.[7] Like the spring on a pinball machine, Procter's expression is pulled back so tightly that it always promises to shoot forth with an overflow of feeling, but instead becomes intensified and protracted because unreleased.[8]

Procter may also have felt her voice to be mediated by the literary circle entertained by her mother, Anne Benson Skepper, a brilliant conversationalist and hostess to Wordsworth, Charles Lamb, Hazlitt, Leigh Hunt, Longfellow, the Rossettis and Coventry Patmore, amongst others. While these luminaries introduced her to the world of letters, they also crowded Procter, who would later reflect on her early environment in her short biography of Juliette Récamier. Writing of this famous French beauty, she declared:

> The very cloud of incense which the great minds and noble hearts who surrounded her offered at her shrine, almost conceals their idol. The interest of her life would at first sight seem to lie rather in the characters of those by whom she was surrounded, than in her own; the genius and the feeling which crowned her would appear not hers, but that of others. And yet we should make a great mistake if we looked upon her as interesting solely, or principally, from having been intimately associated with most of the celebrities of her time. Consciously or unconsciously, she exercised a powerful and enduring influence upon them all.[9]

Procter would prove outstandingly influential upon her contemporaries, who were variously moved by her poetry, as in the case of Dickens and Browning; her religious conviction, the Unitarian Bessie Parkes converting to Roman Catholicism after the counsel of her friend; and her person, Thackerary and Matilda Hays both falling in love with Procter. The following chapter will address her beginnings as a poet and then turn to how religion came to shape the expression within such work. Constantly concerned with the assertion of feeling in poetry, Procter was also committed to philanthropy, as her contributions to the *English Woman's Journal* attest. Such work, coupled with Procter's relationship with Hays, founded her approach to rendering poetical feeling in her final compositions, the outcome of which is discussed in a closing reading of 'A Lost Chord'.

'MARY BERWICK'

'Mary Berwick' was the pseudonym Procter created to mask her poetic identity in her early career, using it to submit poems through a circulating library in London to Charles Dickens's periodical, *Household Words*. Dickens, a friend of the Procter family, assumed the poet behind such verses to be a governess, 'remarkably business-like, punctual, self-reliant, and reliable', and in his excitement at the quality of the work, took some proofs round to show Bryan Procter. 'Next day', Dickens writes in his Introduction, 'brought me the disclosure that I had spoken of the poem to the mother of its writer, in its writer's presence; that I had no such correspondent in existence as Miss Berwick; and that the name had been assumed by Barry Cornwall's eldest daughter, Miss Adelaide Anne Procter.'[10] Why did the young poet strive so rigorously to guard her persona? First, Procter claimed that if she had sent Dickens poems marked with her own name 'that he does not honestly like, either it will be very painful to him to return them, or he will print them for papa's sake, and not for their own'.[11] Second, Procter was wary of her father's thwarted poetical ambition and wanted to avoid overshadowing a talent she deeply respected, confessing to Parkes that 'Papa is a poet. I only write verses'.[12] Both reasons intimate that Procter was confident of her poetical ability, worrying only that Dickens might not 'like' them rather than considering them poor quality; and anxious that she should not be regarded as better than her father. This latter concern intimates the regard Procter had for her father's work, itself part of a school of poetry that privileged the kind of emotional intensity she would come to be celebrated for in her own verse.

Bryan Procter certainly encouraged his daughter's literary pursuits, composing several adoring verses to her from an early age and admiring her later popularity.[13] As a poet, however, he was self-denigrating, taking refuge in his work as a lawyer and Commissioner for Lunacy after his writing was accused of effeminacy and fancy. Like Keats, Bryan Procter was found guilty because of his association with Leigh Hunt, whose polished and emotive style was decried by John Gibson Lockhart in his *Blackwood's* article 'On the Cockney School of

84

Poetry' (1817–19). Yet, from his contributions to the *London Gazette* in 1815 to his perceived role as the leader of a new generation of Hellenistic and mythological poets in the 1820s, Bryan Procter played a significant part in the literary campaign with which Hemans was so involved, namely the preservation of poetry in a culture increasingly dominated by the novel. Concerned professionally with the problem of lunacy, Bryan Procter believed poetry a possible cure, suggesting in 'On English Poetry' (1825) that it is 'the harmony of the mind' which 'embraces and reconciles its seeming discords'.[14] Likewise, in his 'A Defence of Poetry' (1828), Bryan Procter renders poetry a study and reflection upon 'the movements of the human mind, – to see how it is affected by certain causes, and how it adapts itself to various contingencies, – to contemplate it when under extraordinary depression, or when lifted to a state of perilous excitement'.[15] It is not surprising that 'Marcian Colonna' (1820), his portrayal of the fall into madness and the murderous consequences that can ensue, moved Browning to compose 'Porphyria's Lover' (1836). Fascinated by delirium and derangement, then, Bryan Procter was also captured by visions and dream states, as the opening lines of 'The Fall of Saturn: A Vision' (1823) attest:

> I dream – I dream – I dream
> Of shadow and light, – of pleasure and pain,
> Of Heaven, – of Hell: – And visions seem
> Streaming for ever athwart my brain.

> (ll.1–4)

There is a sense of overflow here that is nevertheless contained, the speaker losing himself within fantasy but in control of such loss, the repetition of 'I dream' underlining the authority of the narrative voice. Similarly, the narrator of 'A Vision' (1819) recalls a reverie in which he secures the 'power' to call up the dead: 'and I/ Summoned the spirits', he declares (ll. 25–6). This memory again gives the narrator opportunity to explore his own feelings within the dream state, and for Bryan Procter this was the point of all his verse. For in the Preface to *Dramatic Scenes and other Poems* (1819) he states, 'I have endeavoured to mingle poetic imagery with expressions of natural emotion: but it has been my wish, where the one seemed to jar with the other, that the former should give place to the latter'.[16]

Emotion in poetry was paramount for Procter's father, then, and she too was preoccupied with rendering feeling in her verse. Poetry, as for Hemans and Greenwell, was the prime vehicle for the expression of feeling and Dickens recorded her 'love of poetry' as fervent from 'so early an age, that I have before me a tiny album made of small note-paper, into which her favourite passages were copied for her by her mother's hand before she herself could write. It looks as if she had carried it about, as another little girl might have carried a doll.'[17] Yet this image of Procter clinging protectively onto poetry as a personal comforter intimates her sense that the rendering of feeling should be restrained and not mellifluent, a marked move away from her father's views on verse. Aware of the burden her father, as well as Hemans, had carried for effusing a gushing poetics, she sought instead to depict an equally fervent kind of emotion through a more contained linguistic frame. Hemans's obvious successor, Procter sought to reshape feeling for her own time, wary of appearing too feminized in a period in which such a label was being explored and exploded, not least by her friends at Langham Place. The dismantling of traditional notions of femininity, however, was a process both tentative and fraught, as was Procter's own poetry, betraying as it does her struggle to find a poetic voice. 'Murmurs' (1856), for example, characterizes the speaker's very annunciation as a whispered undertone unable to become fully vocalized; while the narrator implores the reader to 'Listen, and I will tell thee/ The song Creation sings', it is apparent from the description of such a confession that clarity is unobtainable (ll. 13–14). For the 'holy song' the narrator strives to declare is cloaked in shadowy metaphors: it echoes, ripples and glitters in its efforts to be amplified through the 'little voice' of the believer. Compare this to the silent voice of Bryan Procter's 'A Voice' (1820), softly effused and yet entirely voiced, humming and chanting throughout the poem and augmented in the harmonies of 'air-touched harps' (l. 19).

Procter's verse has no such resolution, however faint, 'Incompleteness' (1858) recognizing the unfinished and un-speakable nature of a world created by a higher power, 'God's gifts' marked by 'incompleteness' (l. 25). These gifts, namely the creation, 'roll/ Towards some infinite depth of love and sweetness/ Bearing onward man's reluctant soul', in order to find a place where harmony and wholeness might coexist (ll. 26–8). While for Bryan Procter this place is poetry itself, his daughter deemed such a locale sacred and heavenly, the soul remaining incarcerated within mortal time (ll. 25–8). 'Unexpressed' (1858) conveys the silent nature the soul owns until seated in heaven, the poem a catalogue of varying attempts, all failed, to express what 'Dwells within the soul of every Artist' (l. 1). As Armstrong argues, the poem's message is 'the failure of articulation and the ephemeral nature of language', especially as this relates to the problem of elucidating intangible ideas like the soul, or poetry, or love. The artist figure here, rendered as philosopher, painter, musician and poet, must submit to the fact that 'the best remains unuttered', the 'deepest beauty' always veiled 'to mortal eyes' (ll. 3, 7–8). The implication is that only God has access to the full resonance of what the artist endeavours to fix in form, as the verse focused upon the poet figure conveys:

> No real Poet ever wove in numbers
> All his dreams; but the diviner part,
> Hidden from all the world, spake to him only
> In the voiceless silence of his heart.

(ll. 21–4)

The poet's most profound and thus divine harmonies are too bright for 'the world', murmuring within a still heart that, as the seat of emotion, contains powerful feeling until it is ready to be released in more sacred realms. The narrator's claim that poets cannot weave 'in numbers' all their 'dreams' at once touches upon Procter's cautious approach to the dreamworld as it also recalls the 'tuneless numbers' of 'Ode to Psyche' (1818). Keats's narrator too confesses that his numbers are inharmonious, 'wrung/ By sweet enforcement and remembrance' in a strained venture to address the goddess who represents the soul and so who might release it where Procter finds it bound (ll. 1–2). It is essential for Keats that the poet understand his task to be what Helen Vendler calls a 'conceptualising activity', writing out the imagination in numbers and so doing without the christian input that Procter relies on to illuminate what she cannot, or will not, voice.[18] In other words,

Keats replaces christianity with his own sense of a world that both sensually and creatively forges the soul and so owns it, all abstractions realized within a poetical form that internalizes the intangible, whether it be God or dreams or emotions. Hence the meeting of Psyche and Cupid within the bower of the poet's mind at the end of the Ode and the realization of their love. Not so for Procter, who closes 'Unexpressed' by relating 'Love and Art' as:

> twin mysteries; different, yet the same:
> Poor indeed would be the love of any
> Who could find its full and perfect name.

(ll. 26–8)

The 'secret' of love, and so, by association, art, is so deep that its expression is 'Like sighings of illimitable forests,/ And waves of an unfathomable sea', unreachable by the reader and poet alike (ll. 35–6). Meaning is unravelled only beyond the mortal realm, but unlike Keats and her father, Procter is wary of the dreamworld as a place where such depths can be plummeted. The assurance of heaven is what Procter sought and her considerable aesthetic restraint found this assurance in the religious idea of reserve, one that demanded that the believer deliberately obscure any attempt to describe God's creation in all its variety.

Reserve, as noted in the previous chapter on Greenwell, signifies a holding back of emotion in textual and spoken portrayals of religious subjects and so privileged poetry as an already elusive and reverential genre. Yet the very action of reserving feeling on the page implies the well of emotion behind the language, thus acknowledging the break between feeling and symbol that concerned John Stuart Mill.[19] As Armstrong notes, this kind of emotion remains secret but is 'always pressing for a release': in poetical terms, release cannot be granted, but in religious terms, heaven promises to reveal all and liberate that which is limited on earth. The religious poet precariously balances between the two, her art fit to burst with the feelings it contains, but in existence because of such repression: there is no poetry in heaven for a writer like Procter because such a realm is constituted by the very feelings – love, consolation, passion, comfort and so on – that she desires her poetry to create. The modern fear that we stifle emotion at our peril, then, had little urgency in this period, reliant as it was on God as a regulatory power. Keble, whose essays on poetics deeply touched Procter, may have worried that the poet might go mad in his effort to resist expression, but faithfully depended on divine consolation. Bryan Procter had no such conviction, however. At the beginning of 'Marcian Colonna', for example, the narrator asserts that the earliest Italian poets from whom Colonna descends 'were they who wove/ Thy silken language into tales of love', a far cry from Procter's assertion in 'Unexpressed' that to weave love in verse is nigh impossible without God's intervention. Colonna suffers accordingly. Imprisoned in part one of the poem, 'clouds of madness roll' over him, a 'darker passion' that overflows like powerful feeling but drowns his mind without the barrier reserve provides. Driven finally to murder his lover, Julia, Colonna's emotions are entirely extinguished: 'And frenzy suffered then a silent change,/ And his heart hardened as the fire withdrew/ Like furnaced iron beneath the winter's dew' (st. XV, ll. 38–40). Procter avoids smothering emotion by letting it lie in the undertones of quiet and murmuring phrases, trusting that its overflow will be safely channelled by God.

RELIGION

Gregory begins her study of Procter by stating that her poetry is infused with a deeply religious tone apparent from the earliest of her published poems, 'Ministering Angels' (1843), its concluding 'Leave me not lone to struggle with the world' betraying Procter's dependence on God.[20] Yet her religious faith was more complex, and, while it did not draw on many different belief-systems like Greenwell's, it was variously touched by High Anglicanism, Evangelicalism and Roman Catholicism. As she wrote in a letter to Parkes: 'Each man brings his own bundle of ideas & keeps his own views subordinate of course to the one great moving principle of Religion'.[21] While fundamentally a Roman Catholic poet, nearly all of her verse published after her conversion in 1851, she had been educated in the previous year at F. D. Maurice's

Queen's College, where the Evangelical Charles Kingsley taught. Ferdinand Janku suggests that this intensely anti-Tractarian environment spurred Procter's philanthropic interests through its emphasis upon the values of christian socialism and yet, theologically, this was not a system with which she felt able to associate. Procter instead found the solace she searched for in Roman Catholicism, and the significance of her conversion has been profoundly underestimated by critics. This was a striking and dangerous move in an increasingly anti-Catholic culture, prejudice against those dedicating themselves to a foreign Pope escalating after the passing of the Catholic Emancipation Act in 1829. Yet it was not until 1850, notably the year before Procter's conversion, that Catholicism became seriously regarded as a threat to the Church of England, the Roman hierarchy re-established in England and Wales and led by its distinguished convert, John Henry Newman. As Horton Davies argues, the reaction against the conservatism and indifference of the previous age, culminating as it did in the Romantic movement, also encouraged a general respect for the organic growth of ancient societies and institutions: hence Bryan Procter's fascination with Hellenism. His daughter, however, found her solace in the Roman Catholic renaissance, identifying with its marginalized and often silenced status. As Newman wrote in his famous 'Second Spring' sermon preached in 1852, English Catholics were 'a people who shunned the light of day', seeming 'cut off from the populous world around them, and dimly seen, as if through a mist or in twilight, as ghosts flitting to and fro, by the high Protestants'.[22] Procter would echo this in 'An Appeal: The Irish Church Mission for Converting the Catholics' (1862), Catholicism portrayed as a 'chained and oppressed' church which 'lieth low'; 'Spare her, oh cruel England!' the narrator cries (ll. 1–3). The Oxford Movement had already responded to the nation's distrust of traditional forms of worship coloured by a reserved aesthetics and concern with the mysteries of religion. Serving to popularize mystery and reticence within the practice of the Anglican faith, the Movement also paved the way for an increased tolerance of Roman Catholicism, perceived within Britain as a foreign and preternatural religion. Yet this air of esotericism strongly appealed to Procter and, together with the emphasis upon the powerful figure of the Blessed Virgin Mary and its sense of conviction, Rome appeared to the poet as an alluring spiritual home.

Procter visited Italy between 1853 and 1854, ostensibly to improve her health, but she was already drawn to the country as a seat of Catholicism and poetry alike. Here she stayed with her aunt, Emily de Viry, the younger sister of her mother who had married the Sardinian count, Comte William de Viry, in 1840. Leaving England to live with him in Turin the same year, Aunt Emily had become a devout Catholic and encouraged her niece's faith, which had turned toward the religion at least as early as 1849, the year Parkes disputably pinpoints as that of her conversion. As Parkes asserted: 'In her religious attitude she resembled a foreign rather than an English Catholic. She looked like a Frenchwoman mounting the steps of the Madeleine, or a veiled Italian in St Peters. The one thing she never mentioned was her own conversion.'[23] Parkes's assessment is revealing for two reasons. First, it further attests to Procter's constrained nature, her refusal to mention an event as profound and intensely emotional as a conversion rendering her an ideal candidate for a religion wherein passions ran deep below the surface of the individual and were rarely expressed. Newman was certainly frustrated with what he considered the primary failing of Protestantism, namely its incessant interrogation of the feelings at the expense of actually contemplating God: true faith for him, as for Procter, was not for 'Christians who are taken up in their own feelings, and who describe what they should exhibit'.[24] Nevertheless, Parkes's focus on Procter as a 'spirited' and 'militant' believer is consistent with the notion that she appeared as a 'foreign', and therefore rather passionate, Catholic.[25] This disjunction between Procter's reserved nature and her passionate side was played out in her poetry, as we have seen, and in some ways provides a commentary on the state of Catholicism in England. For English Roman Catholicism was essentially a plain and quiet religion, intent on reviving the faith and culture of a Gothicized medievalism where churches were stylistically utilitarian, vestments simple and the music old Gregorian chant. Yet as the Catholic revival progressed, many confused it with the concurrent fashion for Italian religious taste popularized by High Anglicanism: the most ornate and rit-ualized ceremonial was invariably found in Anglo-Catholic, not Catholic, churches. This mistake was an easy one, especial-ly with figures like Frederick William Faber around, an English Roman Catholic poet and priest who, as Davies suggests, appalled Newman with his 'exotic fashions', 'florid and uninhibitedly passionate prayers' and fervent piety.[26]

Procter was enthralled by Faber, however, and while she appreciated the practical affect Newman forwarded, was quick to recommend Faber's services at the Brompton Oratory.[27] She even wrote to Richard Monckton-Milnes in 1855 warning him that the 'Church is so crowded it would be safe to get there in good time'.[28] Like Procter, Faber had been initially drawn to Tractarianism, but followed Newman into the Roman Catholic Church and was ordained a priest in 1847. Two years later he moved to the Oratory in order to establish poor schools and nightly liturgies for the homeless, maximizing his use of the church domain to create within an at once spiritual and electric atmosphere. Faber enhanced his services further by introduc-ing his own fervently devotional hymns into the ceremony and was widely considered responsible for both instituting and popularizing congregational singing among English Roman Catholics. Yet he was not the only poet to find inspiration for hymns and poetry alike within church walls, Keble's *The Christian Year* (1827) and Christina Rossetti's *Verses* (1893) both good examples of collections that comment variously on the power of the experiential space inside the church and the importance of creating a milieu appropriate to the mysterious and profound nature of worship. Isaac Williams even used the church to structure his sequence *The Cathedral* (1838), prefacing it with references both to Herbert's *The Temple* (1633), 'where moral and sacred Lessons' are attached to church architecture; and to Wordsworth's *The Excursion* (1814), 'being arranged as the parts of a Gothic Church'.[29]

Procter's most successful contribution to this tradition was 'A Tomb in Ghent' (1855), the story of a cathedral organist who dedicates himself to the church and the poor before falling in love with a beautiful musician. The maiden's early death provokes his own, and yet their prior marriage conceives a daughter who begins the narrative, the speaker of the poem captured by the magical tones of her mother's 'murmured' song (l. 8). She then proceeds to relate how her English grandfather arrived in Ghent in the early nineteenth century in search of artisanal work, dwelling 'alone' but for his 'sickly boy' whom he consoled by relating 'strange stories' (ll. 34, 37, 42). The young child enjoys one tale above all, that of the 'gilt dragon' now 'glaring fiercely down/ From the great belfry' of the local St Bavon, a war trophy taken by 'a Crusader from far Palestine/ And given to Bruges' before being stolen by Ghent (ll. 46–50). Informed that 'One day the dragon – so 'tis said – will rise' and fly home, the boy is 'Each day surprised to find it watching there', and, fascinated by the cathedral on which it perches, becomes attached to it as 'his home for rest or play' (ll. 54, 60, 118). The boy finds himself especially enchanted by the White Maiden's Tomb, an angelic statue which seems to sing with the 'organ's pealing music', so directing him to a musical career he fulfils with a 'master-power' (ll. 142, 168). As an adult, he becomes an acclaimed musician 'many came to be/ His pupils in the art of harmony', the speaker declares, but it is love that finally overcomes him, 'His own White Maiden, calm, and pure, and mild' (ll. 188–94). The early death of this human maiden compels him to look beyond mortal reality to 'the midnight of sad skies' and his heart finally breaks upon the White Maiden's Tomb. Our narrating daughter figure is thus left orphaned and forced to return to England to live with strangers, 'kinsmen she had never known' (ll. 251, 259, 279). The poem's close is haunted by the spectre of her dreams of 'Some strange old chant, or solemn Latin hymn/ That echoed through the old cathedral dim', traces of the Belgian cathedral's Roman Catholic ceremony introduced into English territory through the memories of a female poet-narrator (ll. 288–9).

Procter never visited Ghent, and wrote to Bessie Parkes of her 'great wish to go there – greater than for greater places'; yet she had already travelled to the more clearly Catholic Italy and Ghent's artistic and cosmopolitan renown rendered its Catholic heritage more attractive still to the poet.[30] For Gregory, the poem is about Procter's struggle with Tractarianism, her simultaneous desire to implement and refuse its aesthetic devotional ideas, reserve, simplicity of style and typology undermined as they are advocated. Janku too perceives a sense of dissension in the poem's form, rendering it an epic lyric; for, as Susan Stewart suggests, epic conventions generally suit ideological ends while the immediacy of lyric is assumed a counter to such rhetoric or propaganda.[31] 'A Tomb in Ghent' betrays a politicized agenda as Gregory argues, who locates it within Procter's Crimean War poems; but the narrative is much more religiously focused, each of its central motifs – the cathedral, the organ, the dragon, the tomb – inviting the reader into its implicit defence of freedom in religious thought, whether Roman Catholic, Tractarian or otherwise. The narrative is built on contraries, not to insinuate the poet's hesitant relationship to Catholicism, but to forward an almost Blakean vision of faith which empties itself of worldly constraints to aim for a higher way of believing rooted in the imagination. The dragon, for example, has obvious demonic qualities, his vision burning through onlookers and exposing his readiness to forsake Ghent and return to Palestine. Yet the creature is also displaced and homeless and its future escape is near hoped for by the speaker, who foresees the day when it will 'Spread his bright wings, and glitter in the skies' (l. 55).

Similarly, the White Maiden's Tomb is a site of death, repressed emotion and sadness even as the young boy considers it a maternal and welcoming image whose illusory singing invokes a poetry equivalent to prayer and worship. Gregory reads the white maiden as a marker of woman's petrifaction before God, comparing this narrative to Caroline Bowles Southey's 'The Legend of Santarem' (1836) wherein two orphan sisters are turned to stone by the visionary brightness that exudes from Jesus as he visits them inside a cathedral. Yet Procter awakens her white maiden by duplicating her in the body of a real woman, 'her cheek betrayed/ No marble statue, but a living maid', her vocal performance no illusion but filling the cathedral and rendering time itself harmonious: 'How the melodious wingèd hours flew', the speaker declares (ll. 198–9, 219). While the living maid's demise is imminent, she is glorified in the poem for prizing music, poetry, love and God in the moment, a theme to which Procter returns in poems like 'Now' (1853), 'Shining Stars'

(1854) and 'One by One' (1855), each underlining the importance of seizing the present instant. The narrator of 'Now', for
example, insists that the reader 'Rise' from both 'dreams of the
Future' and the 'phantom arms' of the past in order to embrace
what is immediate and real, namely one's union with God (ll.
1, 9, 22). Such a union can only take place within a dream,
vision or imaginative space and so for Procter it is the
believer's daily dream of God that is most pressing for us to
conjure within the artistic space. Again Procter recalls Blake in
his declaration that 'Vision or Imagination is a Representation
of what Eternally Exists. Really & Unchangeably', rather than
memories of the past or allegorical stories.[32] Indeed, the legend
of 'A Tomb in Ghent' serves only to render such ideas in more
basic terms than those Blake opted for, and it is Procter's vision
of the interior spiritual space the church provides that shines
from the poem. The emphasis is upon the reader's sensual
perception of the church space as one wherein reverie is made
spiritual through the imagination, and the actual aesthetic
quality of the cathedral's material architecture becomes sec-
ondary.[33] For the 'carved angels', 'marble saint[s]' and 'demon-
heads grotesque' of Procter's cathedral are made ghostly and
ethereal by 'silver clouded incense' and illuminated by the
'blazoned glory' of the glowing stained-glass 'Archangels' by
day, and the 'lamps that gleamed' like 'sparks of fire' or
'trembling stars' by night (ll. 65–117). This vision recalls
Faber's impassioned Catholicism as much as Blake's anti-
materialism, and ultimately Procter uses the poem as a
platform to forward a profoundly Roman aesthetic, as well as
message, to her Anglican readership.

Procter's emphasis upon the supernatural and intangible
elements of Catholicism also found expression in her poems on
the Blessed Virgin Mary, who is recalled in the statue of the
White Maiden which continues to glow even after the other
players depart the scene. It is the eerie tunes that strangely
issue from her marble lips that the young girl carries with her
to England, just as Procter returned from Italy enchanted by
the figure of the Virgin. Her fascination was fuelled further by
the vehement Faber who claimed of Mary, 'How like a priest
she seems!', the very 'strength of the Church, the queen of the
apostles', and at least a third of Procter's religious collection *A*

Chaplet of Verses (1862) are devoted to Mary.[34] The Virgin held an iconic appeal for Procter, a ghostly yet serene presence that seemed to embody a reserved and yet intense form of emotion that linked human and spiritual feeling together. 'Links with Heaven', for example, serves to underline Mary's human aspect, regarding her as a mother who impels the children of heaven to pray in turn for their mothers. Yet by capitalizing pronouns which refer to Mary, Procter endows her with a Christ-like status, stressing her distance from the individual as one who must be worshipped and invoked within prayer. 'The Annunciation' and 'Evening Chant' each command the reader to celebrate and honour Mary, where 'Christmas Flowers' reads like a mini christian-year guide to the Assumption, her purification and the birth of Christ. Procter often uses poems as spaces to teach readers how to start to think about Catholicism too, an unfamiliar religion to many and one which had been branded as theologically deranged when set against Anglicanism. While the communal church-going aspect of the latter faith infused middle-class England, Procter believed, like Greenwell, that it lacked the spiritual power of Catholicism, which she attempted to communicate through her invocations of Mary.[35] Decorating these poems with Ave Marias, Hail Marys, Gloria Patris and Ora Pro Mes, the foreign off-beat tone of the language seems designed to ease the reader into a different way of approaching God, one based primarily on the visionary. Procter executes such a task in 'The Shrines of Mary', picturing memorials devoted to the Virgin the world over as a constellation of stars 'bright with heavenly radiance' and alive 'like mystical flowers' (ll. 7, 9). The organic glowing rays of these shrines issue from old chapels, vast cathedrals and lonely altars alike, weaving together 'like a garland' that the subject might wrap around his or her heart (ll. 11). Symbolically pulling 'the Heart of Mary' within the self, then, the subject can experience the Virgin's momentous emotional capacity to feel both dejection, 'Our Lady of Sorrows', and jubilation, the 'Queen of Heaven' (ll. 119, 142, 180).

'A Legend of Provence' (1859) draws the reader even closer to Mary, presenting her as a redemptive force with the power to lift mortals into a dreamlike realm transcendent of earthly temptation. The legend of the poem concerns a young novice,

Angela, who is lured into a worldly romance by a knight whom she nurses in the convent. Once outside the clean tranquillity of the cloister walls, the nun's dreams fade and she is abandoned by the knight, her only fate that of the 'outcast', scorned by society as a now corrupt woman (l. 203). Plunged into the depths of despair, the nun is suddenly transfixed by 'a radiance bright', enfolding her within a 'strange and sudden light', as Mary appears as a ghostly vision (ll. 258–9). As Angela entreats the vision for assistance, Mary answers:

> 'From thy bitter past,
> Welcome, my child! oh, welcome home at last!
> I filled thy place. Thy flight is known to none,
> For all thy duties I have done;
> Gathered thy flowers, and prayed, and sung, and slept;
> Didst thou not know, poor child, *thy place was kept*?'
>
> (ll. 263–71)

Assuming the persona and physical being of Angela within the convent, Mary becomes momentarily human, intimating a make-up of the self which remains mysterious and supernatural. The narrative frame, uttered by Angela in a moment of recollection, also emphasizes the immaterial elements of being and suggests that it is our intangible qualities – faith, hope, love and so on – that are more profoundly real than our often misguided actions. Such musing is itself sparked by a spooky portrait of Mary the reader watches the nun contemplate as the poem opens, lit up like a 'Rembrandt' and effusing a 'mystic gloom' that provokes the telling of the legend (ll. 10, 17). Foreshadowing Freud's declaration, 'When you think of me, think of Rembrandt; a little light and a great deal of darkness', Procter too encourages the reader to embrace the unknown, of both the self and God.[36] While reserving one's faith allows a calmer contemplation of religious matters, so submitting to the veiled parts of the self paradoxically leads to self-realization: as Angela states at the end of her tale, the 'hopes that lost in some far distance seem/ May be the truer life, and this the dream' (ll. 335–6). By shaking off the fetters of the physical body, the subject is 'redeemed from death' and becomes more profoundly vital through the spirit: it is not the dreamworld that Procter privileges here, but the necessity of embracing the immaterial – the inner life of emotion and faith – over and above that of the material.

A SOCIAL CONSCIENCE

Procter's elevation of the spirit, however, did not detract from her desire to help the underprivileged in more palpable terms. She donated the money raised from sales of the *Chaplet* to Father Daniel Gilbert's Providence Row Night Refuge for Homeless Women and Children, opened in 1860 with the support of the Sisters of Mercy in East London. Moving later to larger premises in Spitalfields, the shelter was the first to offer sanctuary to homeless Catholics, and Procter's involvement with it is exemplary of the manner by which her religious faith spurred her philanthropic activities. Indeed the *Chaplet* contained many of her most socially vital poems, 'Homeless', 'The Homeless Poor', 'Our Titles' and 'A Beggar' powerfully critiquing hierarchized conceptions of the class system in Britain as well as society's refusal to deal with poverty. Dickens even thought that Procter's obsession with social issues contributed to her early death and, as Kate Flint argues, he was notoriously opposed to women involving themselves with 'causes', attacking what he called 'bloomerism' in his charmingly titled paper 'Sucking Pigs' (1851).[37] This did not stop him from printing many of Procter's more socially concerned poems in *Household Words*, however, a two-penny miscellany dedicated to 'the discussion of the most important social questions of the time'.[38] Stressing both 'Instruction and Entertainment' for a middle-class, family-based audience, Dickens insisted in a letter to Elizabeth Gaskell that the 'general mind and purpose' of his periodical was 'the raising up of those that are down, and the general improvement of our social condition'.[39] The journal freely addressed problems of poverty, homelessness, sanitation and health, criminality, slum life and illiteracy, and advocated a national system of public education consisting of free schooling for the poor. It became a veritable whistleblower, raising questions concerning safety in factory work, hierarchy in the armed forces, nepotism in the civil service, injustice in the prison system, the misuse of charity funds, the perplexities of the law and Government neglect of slavery, war crimes, debt and women's rights. Inviting the public to discuss these abuses by presenting them in accessible articles and poems, *Household Words* also provided enough entertainment to keep readers focused, general pieces on topical news items, art, music, cookery, natural history, the sciences and so on, rendering it a predecessor of our own weighty weekend newspapers. Yet it remained literary in disposition, many editions dominated by the work of Dickens and his fellow editor, Wilkie Collins, and the Christmas numbers of the journal including stories and poems that might be communally read aloud in family sitting rooms.

While Procter's work accounted for about a sixth of the total number of poems published in *Household Words*, her contributions to the Christmas numbers, which ran between 1850 and 1858, most readily map her struggle to develop an at once religious and political voice.[40] These seasonal editions reached an extraordinary circulation of around 250,000 and consisted of a series of stories by various authors grouped together within a narrative framework written by Dickens or Collins. As the only poet within the sequences, Procter occupied a pivotal position, the compact and measured appearance of her verses directing the reader to key points she believed, or Dickens considered, central to the theme.[41] 'The Angel's Story', for example, the fourth piece in the 1853 Christmas number, 'Another Round of Stories by the Christmas Fire', tackles issues of child poverty amidst the newly industrialized London. For all the opportunity London offered, it also propagated an underside of diseased and impoverished communities crammed into poor housing, as Procter's narrator claims in despair: 'The skill of all that mighty City/ To save one little life was vain' (ll. 38–9). Even the rich fall prey to disease, as the young victim who lies dying from stanza 5 portrays, his 'costly toys' lying 'unheeded' and his mother powerless to offer relief, suffering with him and 'Murmuring tender song and story/ Weary hours to beguile' (ll. 49–50). Like Procter's more personal narrative voice, the mother's inflection is quiet and whispering, her own reserved faith obliquely calling up the 'unseen Presence' who hovers 'radiant' in the following stanza (ll. 51, 57). The angel, 'slowly rising', sweeps the child up into a tour of the poorest districts of the city, taking him back into the past to focus on a 'little sickly orphan' (l. 89). This sick child, 'his baby spirit' weighed down by 'Grim Want' and 'Sorrow', finds refuge in the 'princely halls and mansions' of our angel-born sufferer, who is reminded of his own tenderness towards the orphaned child (ll. 95–8). Losing the 'holy dreams of childhood', the penniless infant is given divine solace in heaven, and granted the office of angel in order to seek out the richer youth who once extended such sympathy (l. 162). Only the *Legends and Lyrics* copy of the poem offers a final verse in which the two boys are buried side by side, the unmarked pauper's grave appearing as humble and sanctified as the grandiose marble tomb of the affluent child. The bond between them is almost necessarily hidden, rendered sacred by its omission from the *Household Words* edition and without any narrative realization: for in one sense, it is the very communication between the two boys at the gated boundary between their worlds that infects and finally kills them both.

In a different way, the boys also save each other from a cruel adult world and Procter's social poems often tread the precarious territory between material commentary and a longing for the heavenly beyond. Procter continued to address this tension in her other Christmas-number offerings, 'The Sailor Boy' and 'A Legend of Bregenz', both appearing in the 1854 edition, 'The Seven Poor Travellers'. As Gregory argues, the two poems set alongside each other convey Procter's alternately repressed and expressive poetical voice, and her political critique is often shrouded in the misty religious tenor her work persistently forwards.[42] 'The Sailor Boy', for example, reads in a curtailed and truncated manner, its compressed metre complicating the feelings that run between the orphaned sea-bound child and the adoptive mother figure of the Countess, which remain central but are never effused. Compare this with Hemans's 'The Adopted Child', wherein the protagonist passionately struggles to discover his biological family, and Procter's young speaker appears oddly measured and still in his response to the relationships he both forges and loses. 'The Legend of Bregenz', on the other hand, reads as if part of the *Records of Woman* (1828), the effusive story of an Austrian woman's exile and determined return to protect her home town from attack.

Dickens began to comment on the nature of Procter's lyrical tone in the 1855 Christmas number, 'The Holly Tree Inn', casting her as a 'Barmaid' who narrates a tale 'which went so pleasantly to the music of her voice, that I ought rather to say it turned itself into verse, than was turned into verse by me'.[43] Intimating that Procter's poem magically transforms into a lyrical production without the intrusion of an author or editor, Dickens is almost dismissive of the intense and unusual expressivity of this particular lyric, one that reaches far greater emotional heights than the number's other contributions. The story recounts the love Maurice, the young inhabitant of the inn, develops for a 'damsel' who stops periodically at his resting place in order that her 'train of horsemen' might pause for shelter (ll. 37, 43). At first, she appears happy and her laughter rings 'Like silver on the air', illuminating the shady inn, overshadowed as it is by 'apple-branches' and a towering 'Judas Tree' (ll. 15–16, 72). Pulling down the 'fairst blossom' from this foliage, the young boy presents the damsel with an efflorescent love-token and yet, because this token is symbolically taken from a tree signifying betrayal, the recipient cannot return his affection (l. 67). Her following visits are tainted by an increasing sense of tragedy, as she appears married, then dejected, aged and ill, and finally as part of her own funeral train; the Judas Tree dies with her after its final bloom is removed to adorn the damsel's coffin. Significantly, however, Maurice's passion remains youthful and strong as does he, his homage to the damsel characteristically 'silent' in Procterian terms, but the 'pitying tender sorrow' that lives within his heart a prominent and moving marker of authentic feeling. Procter's reserve mingles with the kind of lyric expressivity Tennyson betrayed in *In Memoriam* (1850), soliloquizing as he does on the virtues of risking all in love, it being 'sweeter to be drunk with loss' than imprisoned by the caution of denial (sect. I, l. 11).

Procter's faith in human love steadily crumbled in her last contributions to the Christmas numbers, however, the 1856 'The Wreck of the Golden Mary' including her profoundly sad 'Homeward Bound'. Prefaced by Dickens's decree that it is a 'curious sort of tuneful no-tune', the reader is immediately alerted to the poem's fraught expression:

for its lyrical musicality broadcasts such raw feeling that the narrator doubts both his resolve and his ability to relate the events that transpired.[44] The poem aches with the unbearable anguish of the narrator, a shipwrecked sailor who spends his lifetime struggling to return home to his wife and child. His narration is one of extreme suffering, reeling between hope and despair but always focused on the 'tender vision' of his home and family which cushions his 'not quite broken' heart (ll. 41, 47). Thrown into 'strange and foreign' localities or overwhelmed by the seemingly boundless oceans, the sailor's array of emotions are at once exposed on the page and distanced from the reader by his measured monologue. Procter's conviction in feeling seems to fail in the figure of the sailor as his moments of feigned calm, desperate hope, torturous dreams and impassioned breakdowns ring empty, all emotion numbed by the weight of sadness the poem carries. For, as the narrator reaches the harbour of his home, his 'sick heart throbbing' to be reunited with his family, he is confronted with the death of his child and a wife who has remarried. Procter defers the moment of realization continually throughout the poem, hinting at tragedy but pulling the reader away from it even when revelation seems imminent. It is as if, like the sailor, the reader is expected to find the truth too biting and the narrator seems physically removed from the scene, 'dead' to the new familial unit. While it is the non-vocal whimpering of 'Tears alone' that dominates the closing stanzas, Procter insists on betraying the acid trace false feeling leaves: 'Bitter tears that desolate moment,/ Bitter, bitter tears we wept', the narrator iterates (ll. 201–2, 205). Reserve triumphs as words neglect to articulate the ardency of this scene and yet the reader is left only with the sailor's devastation and shock amidst broken love.

The theme of faithless and futile love continued to haunt Procter's last Christmas-number poem, 'Three Evenings in the House' (1858), narrated by the desolate Jarber, whom Dickens deems a 'sadly discomposed' man, 'terribly harassed' and 'really quite a spectacle of feebleness and fatigue'.[45] 'What I have gone through,' Jarber declares, 'words are not eloquent enough to tell', introducing the reader to Procter's poem by disavowing the capacity for language to relate suffering.[46] More than simply melancholic, the poem is inharmonious and acrid in tone, and relates the social downfall of a single woman damaged by familial constraint and duty. It is possible that Procter herself was suffering from a romantic struggle around this time: Thackeray speculated in a letter to his daughters Anne and Harriet that 'Adelaide is going to be married'.[47] Thackeray tentatively pursued Procter himself, as did the publisher George Smith under the watchful encouragement of Charlotte Brontë, and yet the poet never married, turning her energies, ostensibly, to philanthropic work.[48] Yet 1858 not only marked Procter's final contribution to *Household Words* and possible separation from a mystery lover, but it also saw the publication of *Legends and Lyrics* and the launch of the *English Woman's Journal*.[49] Procter even dedicated *Legends and Lyrics* to one of the journal's editors, Matilda M. Hays, addressing the love poem 'A Retrospect' (1858) to her, their romantic relationship freeing her from the despair indirectly disclosed in her final *Household Words* poems.[50] Certainly the cross-dressing 'Max' Hays was a notoriously seductive figure, writing a radically anti-marriage novel, *Helen Stanley* (1846), editing George Sand, and forming ardent and sexual friendships with several women, including Charlotte Cushman, Harriet Hosmer and Theodosia Monson.[51] Even Bessie Parkes seems to have fallen for Hays, whom she addressed as 'Matthew' and probably introduced to Procter. As the poet cheekily signed off in a letter to Parkes predating her own engagement with 'Max': 'Remember me to Miss Hays. Has she left your costume at all more ladylike than it was?'[52] What Hays unleashed in Procter may have loosened her emotional responses to poetical subjects, but her influence appears to have also rendered her a sharper, wittier and in the end more cynical writer. Before turning to this darker side of Procter, however, it is necessary to place such a shift within the context of the *English Woman's Journal*, home of her final poems and essays.

THE *ENGLISH WOMAN'S JOURNAL*

Procter's involvement with public causes was rooted in her work for the *English Woman's Journal*, founded at 19 Langham Place in London and attracting a wide circle of political female readers.[53] Publishing articles on similar issues to that of *Household Words* but with a focus on women's issues, the journal invoked several significant changes in employment law, sanitation standards and education. A year after the journal was founded, Procter and Parkes established the Association (later Society) for Promoting the Employment of Women, intended 'for girls and young women, where they may be specially trained to work in shops by being thoroughly well instructed in accounts, book-keeping etc.'[54] While a successful employment register was instituted, the printing profession remained adamant in its refusal of women apprentices, provoking Emily Faithfull, the Society's secretary, to begin the Victoria Press in 1860. The Press was immediately successful, its appointment as Printer and Publisher in Ordinary to Queen Victoria an entitlement which led to the instigation of the *Victoria Magazine*. Faithfull also sought a platform on which she might show off the skills attained by her female compositors and so developed the idea of an anthology of poetry and prose to be edited by Procter. *The Victoria Regia: A Volume of Original Contributions in Poetry and Prose* was issued in 1861, merging Faithfull's ardent politics, manifested in her preface to the book, with Procter's emphasis upon emotion, many of the poems included stressing the power of feeling within an unstable and culturally precarious society. Thus the honeyed resonances of Hays, Tennyson, Arnold, Leigh Hunt, Hemans's friend Henry Chorley, Mary Howitt and 'Barry Cornwall' fused with the politicized tones of Parkes, Harriet Martineau, Trollope and Anna Jameson. Significantly, the Press began to publish the *English Woman's Journal* from 1860 and so further cemented the ties between politics and art, which in turn Procter's contributions illuminated.

The connection between politics and art was explored by Procter in three prose pieces written for the journal, 'A Visit to a Watch-Making Factory' (1859), 'In Search of Solitude' (1859) and 'Madame Récamier' (1860–61), each addressing gritty subjects poetically. 'A Visit' is characteristically lyrical and focuses on the intricate skills of tradeswomen working in a Dorset factory, the process of shaping rusted wires into riveted steel chains evincing an almost aesthetic appeal for Procter.

'Solitude', in comparison, mocks the solitary aesthetic Victorian society had mistakenly come to associate with Wordsworth, undermining the middle-class taste for 'rustic' travels. Procter implicitly assails the fashion, popular with privileged city dwellers, for plunging into travel as a way of experiencing nature and regional difference with little awareness of the pretension of the approach. The paper follows two young women, 'female Timons', who flee 'away into the wilds of Yorkshire' to escape the noise and ugliness of civilized London.[55] The narration is acutely sardonic, the women 'quite anxious that a few very select and rustic and utterly unsophisticated natives should people the moors whither we were going, so as to make the solitude seem still more impressive'.[56] The two friends fit themselves out in 'rustic (and we hoped not unbecoming) costume' and take only the most 'solid' of reading matter, Wordsworth, Browning, Ruskin, Goethe, Carlyle and Tennyson, all left unread but nevertheless adorning their country cottage.[57] Frustrated at first with the towns they pass through for seeming 'too civilised', the women at last reach the most lonely place they can find in order to talk unhindered 'of animated and highly intellectual' subjects.[58] Yet the weight of their reading matter begins literally to anchor them within nature, which fast becomes 'diabolical', not in sublimity, but because of its proliferation of midges; the women return, weary and disillusioned, to 'that real solitude of London'.[59]

Despite the cutting humour Procter evinces here, the central message is a solemn one, attesting to the loneliness of city life and consequent invasion of nature by the middle classes. Procter was aware that the new wealth enabling such travel had been produced by capitalism and industrialization, the very terrors that threatened to extinguish the consolatory solitude nature had offered poets like Wordsworth.[60] It is not by chance that the friends who feature in 'Solitude' take *The Excursion* for holiday reading, a profoundly important poem for Victorian readers because of its creation of an experiential, emotional space in which to take refuge from the world. Procter, like Greenwell, admired the poem for offering spiritual guidance and imaginative relief outside of any doctrinal system and her essay critiques, not Wordsworthian philosophy, but what she perceived as the exploitation of it by an unthinking bourgeoisie. For solitude was not only necessary as a salvific remedy in times of precarious social and cultural change, but it was also essential to enable one to think and write about such change. Procter argued as much in her short biography of Juliette Récamier, published in three parts in the *English Woman's Journal* and conveying sympathy with a figure almost imprisoned by polite society. Married at 15 to the banker, Jacques Récamier, Juliette's 'incontestable' beauty and social position granted her Paris salon an allure that enraptured the most prestigious literary and political crowds of the day.[61] Procter's admiration for her, however, is instead focused on Récamier's final remove to 'an independent apartment in the Convent of the Abbaye au Bois', away from her somewhat scandalous flirtations with the likes of Chateaubriand, Lucien Bonaparte and the Duc de Montmorency. Indeed, describing the interior of the conventual retreat, Procter quotes from Chateaubriand's recollections of a space furnished with nothing more than a 'bookcase, a harp, a piano' and a 'portrait of Madame de Staël'.[62] De Staël's death in 1817 devastated Récamier, who, while considered incapable of forming serious attachments to her lovers, exhibited a profound and arguably romantic commitment to her female friend.[63] Writing of their first encounter, which Procter quotes fully, Récamier declares: 'I was struck by the beauty of her eyes and of her expression; I scarcely understood what I felt [. . .] I blushed; my confusion was excessive [. . .] I expressed what I was feeling by my looks rather than by my words: she both terrified and attracted me at the same moment. [. . .] At that time it was but a vision in my life, but the impression left was very deep. I thought of nothing but Madame de Staël, so profoundly had I felt the attraction of this strong and ardent nature.'[64]

Procter's vibrant intimation of Récamier's relationship with de Staël throws into sharp relief the isolation the salon belle felt at the end of her life, the very note on which the biography closes. 'Speaking one day of happiness,' Procter sorrowfully declares of Récamier, 'she said with a sigh that her ideal was, and always had been, "a happy marriage".'[65] Récamier's inability to find security in love finds an uneasy parallel in

Procter's last poems, published in the *English Woman's Journal* and attesting to a search for passion that is momentarily found and immediately lost with devastating consequence. It has already been noted that the poet's relationship with Hays liberated her emotional being, mirroring Récamier's bond with de Staël but in a magnified manner, the reserved Procter a little overwhelmed by the 'morally loose' reputation of her seductress. Certainly Parkes and Emily Davies were wary of their colleague's lack of propriety and yet it may have been precisely this that so attracted Procter in her search for something other than the normativeness of middle-class life.[66] Drawn to the foreign cathedrals of Belgium and the religious climes of Rome, Procter also felt an outsider to marriage, gloomily reporting on a Piedmontese betrothal party in a letter cited by Dickens and Charles Bruce. 'A most melancholy affair it was,' Procter begins, 'the bridegroom "decidedly tipsy" and the bride "sobbing so, she could hardly stand," finally dragged off between her brother and uncle, with a last explosion of pistols.'[67] The affair is presented by Procter as at once tragic and miserable, made more ugly still by the intervention of belligerent and gun-toting male relatives who cart off the bride to an already debauched husband. The poet knew well that love was a fragile phenomenon, citing a short passage from Emerson at the beginning of *Legends and Lyrics* to convey as much: 'Our tokens of love are for the most part barbarous. Cold and lifeless, because they do not represent our life. The only gift is a portion of thyself' – that which Procter found most hard to give away.[68]

Arguably, the poem which most expressively exposes the self in the volume is 'A Retrospect', a love poem addressed to Hays and a tribute to the pleasure that has arisen from their union amidst a life dominated by grief and listlessness. From a 'fair point of present bliss/ Where we together stand', the poet looks back into a past in which the lover was absent, a 'long and desert land' where 'thou were not' (ll. 1–6). She is physically animated by the newfound presence of the lover, the emotions that mapped out her past suddenly activated in a more assured manner and so offering the poet a fusion of love and security. Each mark of dynamic feeling in the poem – the beating heart, rolling clouds, sweeping of time, dream-effusing soul and grief-stricken visions – pale and freeze when set before the deeper bond that she celebrates with her lover: 'I know now that her heart and mine were waiting,/ Love to welcome thine', the poet declares (ll. 41–2). The past itself disappears, belonging now to the lover whom the narrator readily worships, perceiving that 'even that faded Past/ Was thine, belovèd one', and promising to 'rejoice' that her life is now 'all consecrated, dear,/ to thee' (ll. 45–8). Recalling the tone Christina Rossetti's love poems to Christ evoke, Procter elevates the covenant lovers are able to forge as a direct route to strong emotion: for the relationship envisioned here, whether it is mapped back onto the past or viewed from a current moment, becomes a stage on which both women might feel. While such expressivity is rare for Procter, the poems she contributed to the *English Woman's Journal* and later added to the second edition of *Legends and Lyrics* (1861) betray yet another twist in her poetic development, both reserved and raw in their presentation of feeling and, above all, profoundly sad. What happened to inhibit the joy of poems like 'A Retrospect' (1858) and induce the composition of 'Loss and Gain' (1859) or 'Requital' (1860) is unknown. We might conjecture an unresolved sense of anguish related to the mysterious suitor of whom Thackeray wrote; or turn instead to the by no means constant Hays, who, for all her allure, was perhaps too flighty for the earnest poet.

Hays certainly seems to have unleashed an edginess in Procter that her 1860 poem 'Requital' reflects, the story of a child angel who visits the house of a fallen woman, 'With the brand upon her/ Of want and sin' (ll. 45–6). The scene is set amidst a stormy tempest which, in obscuring the moon and stars, clouds over the 'rays of light' that provide the ladders on which angels move between heaven and earth (l. 12). The angel of this poem is thus trapped in the mortal realm for the night, and so searches for a place to stay until the storm settles. Beating her wings at the windows of various houses, she is refused by them all as an apparition or dream, and only the 'weary' prostitute of the most humble of the dwellings welcomes her inside (l. 43). Drying off her feathers and embracing her maternally, the fallen woman figure is an expression of tenderness and pity; and yet when morning comes, the angel flees 'Up the first sunbeam', having planted a kiss of death upon her hostess (l. 57). It is as if the older female figure atones for her apparent sins through the child angel, the requital of the title perhaps. Yet, as Gregory argues, the verb 'to requite' also implies a sense of quiescence and silence in which the fallen woman is framed: compassionate and reserved, her serenity outshines the angel's babyish conceit.[69] For the angel is painted darkly as a noisy and irresponsible creature, losing herself on earth and battering her wings loudly to gain attention: even her lips seem to punch her venomous kiss deafeningly onto the older woman. While breaking out of the reserved tone she adopts in poems like 'A Tomb in Ghent', Procter's message here is a simple one regarding the deadliness of blaringly pretty surfaces.

The flamboyantly debutante veneer of her own sweetheart may have at first enthralled Procter, but she would later discover the cruelty behind it, Hays betraying her with Theodosia Monson in 1862. As Procter ruefully wrote that year in a letter to Parkes: 'I have been hearing from Lady M.' and 'am quite clear what she intends & means with regard to M.'[70] Protective of their friend, Parkes and Barbara Bodichon pushed Hays to resign from the English Woman's Journal and Procter's family too refused to let her visit the poet when she lay dying two years later.[71] While Procter at first insisted there was no 'necessity for Miss Hays leaving the Editorship' of the Journal, she would later declare that Hays 'was right I think in resigning – & as to the effect I don't care'.[72] Such indifference to her former lover was underlined further by memories of the Saturday Review's infamous and damaging admonishment of the Langham Place reading room as a site of 'very naughty reading', a criticism sparked by Hays's hollow romantic intrigues.[73] Procter's newfound mistrust of beauty's façade may also have threatened her faith, Catholicism's magical atmosphere recalling the disingenuous spell Hays had cast: flimsy and false, if charming. 'Loss and Gain' (1859) had hinted at such fears, but it is the melodic 'A Lost Chord' (1860) that perhaps embodies Procter's struggle with faith, love, authentic feeling and, crucially, the manner by which such subjects might be conveyed.

A LOST CHORD

'A Lost Chord' was composed as Procter worked on her biography of Récamier and betrays a troubled mix of reserve and expressivity that recalls the jammed pinball spring metaphor with which this chapter opened. For in suggesting that emotion will be released within her poetry, but then intensifying such emotion by holding it back, Procter leaves feeling arrested between a state of withdrawal and overflow. Feeling becomes a nebulous and uncertain quality as a consequence, figured as a musical chord the narrator, quite by chance, brings forth while casually jingling out notes on the church organ:

> I do not know what I was playing,
> Or what I was dreaming then;
> But I struck one chord of music,
> Like the sound of a great Amen.
>
> It flooded the crimson twilight
> Like the close of an Angel's Psalm,
> And it lay on my fevered spirit
> With a touch of infinite calm.

(ll. 5–12)

The chord has no precise origin, the narrator forgetting the context of its production: it is simply struck, as a feeling is, emerging powerfully to flood the church but uncontrollable and indistinct. Feeling does not overflow, however, the chord gently suspended on the narrator's spirit to calm and comfort her, like the 'sound of a great Amen'. It is everything that the narrator's practical life is not, an antidote to her fever and a 'harmonious echo' of the discordance of existence, linking 'all perplexèd meanings/ Into one perfect peace' (ll. 15, 17–18). For all the uncertainty surrounding its expression, once tuned in, feeling literally smoothes out conflicts within the self without repressing them, the friction of life recalled and resonating through a newly formed way of being that is both consolatory and replenishing. By bringing together all aspects of existence into a state of completion, the feeling evoked momentarily mirrors Hemans's affection, fusing feeling and thought together to produce a balanced and benevolent individual. Yet Procter's narrator does not possess the faith Hemans's speakers own, and while her perfect chord rings out through the church as a deluge of religious feeling, it quickly fades and vanishes:

> I have sought, but I seek it vainly,
> That one lost chord divine,
> Which came from the soul of the Organ,
> And entered into mine.

(ll. 21–4)

The sense of feeling slipping away or becoming unobtainable even while it resides somewhere inside of us is one that prefigures the development of the Freudian unconscious and yet it remains a theological issue here. Only death or heaven own the necessary means to amplify the chord again, the narrator claims in the closing stanza, underlining the bond between musicality or lyric form and its emotive expression in religious themes. As Hemans declared in 'The Sacred Harp' (1833) and Greenwell in 'Poets' (1861), God is what allows feeling to resonate through the self, whether this feeling be publicly gushed or privately unravelled. Procter is more cautious regarding her dependence upon a divine figure, however, her narrator finally retreating back into herself to await a replay of her chord in a future space. Reserving her feelings, rather than deriding, fearing or playing with them as her modernist legatees would do, Procter ends up bearing the weight of emotion internally rather than externalizing it aesthetically on the page. When Procter became fatally ill from exhaustion in 1864, Dickens worried that she remained too active in her charitable works, although he admitted that she 'must exercise' them, 'or be killed by the restraint'.[74] It is perhaps the restraint of her poetry that kills the feelings declared within for many modern readers. Yet if we come to regard the nature of such utterance in terms of its relationship with religion, Procter might be more readily understood as a poet of feeling, 'not knowing or believing or thinking', betraying a poetical identity recognizable into the twentieth century and beyond.[75]

111

Notes

CHAPTER 1. INTRODUCTION

1. e e cummings, 'A Poet's Advice to Students', in *e. e. cummings: A Miscellany Revised*, ed. George J. Firmage (New York: October House, 1965), 335.
2. Madame de Staël, *Corinne, or Italy*, trans. Sylvia Raphael (1807; Oxford: Oxford University Press, 1998), 147.
3. Letitia Elizabeth Landon, 'On the Character of Mrs Hemans' Writings', *New Monthly Magazine*, 44 (1835), in Jerome McGann and Daniel Riess, *Letitia Elizabeth Landon: Selected Writings* (Ontario: Broadview, 1997), 173–86 (173).
4. Mary Wollstonecraft, *A Vindication of the Rights of Woman*, ed. Mary Warnock (1792; London: Everyman, 1985); and see any of the dialogues between Emma Courtney and Augustus Harley in *Memoirs of Emma Courtney*, ed. Eleanor Ty (1796; Oxford: Oxford University Press, 2000); and *The Love Letters of Mary Hays 1779–1780*, ed. A. F. Wedd (London: Methuen, 1925).
5. The neglect of 'feeling' in current critical discourse has been recently addressed in several important studies, see Isobel Armstrong, *The Radical Aesthetic* (Oxford: Blackwell, 2000); Lauren Berland (ed.), *Compassion: Papers from the English Institute 2000* (London: Routledge, 2003); Elizabeth Fay (ed.), 'Romantic Passions', *Romantic Circles Praxis Series* (April 1998), www.rc.umd.edu/praxis/; Philip Fisher, *The Vehement Passions* (Princeton: Princeton University Press, 2002); John D. Morillo, *Uneasy Feelings: Literature, the Passions and Class: From Neoclassicism to Romanticism* (New York: AMS Press, 2001); Martha Nussbaum, *Upheavals of Thought: The Intelligence of Emotions* (Cambridge: Cambridge University Press, 2001); Adela Pinch, *Strange Fits of Passion: Epistemologies of Emotion: Hume to Austen* (Stanford: Stanford University Press, 1996); Gesa Stedman,

Stemming the Torrent: Expression and Control in the Victorian Discourses on Emotions, 1830–1872 (Aldershot: Ashgate, 2002); and Rei Terada, *Feeling in Theory: Emotion after the 'Death of the Subject'* (Cambridge, MA: Harvard University Press, 2001).

6. See Leslie Stephen, *The Life of Sir James Fitzjames Stephen* (London: Smith, Elder and Co., 1895).

7. Hannah More, *Coelebs in Search of a Wife* (1809; Bristol: Thoemmes Press, 1995), 13.

8. Anna Barbauld, 'Thoughts on the Devotional Taste, On Sects, and on Establishments' (1775), in *Anna Letitia Barbauld: Selected Poetry and Prose*, ed. William McCarthy and Elizabeth Kraft (Ontario: Broadview, 2002), 209–34 (211).

9. Barbauld, 'Thoughts on the Devotional Taste,' 211, 217–18.

10. From a review of *Tales, and Historic Scenes*, in the *Edinburgh Monthly Review*, 2 (August 1819), 194–209, in Gary Kelly (ed.), *Felicia Hemans: Selected Poems, Prose and Letters* (Ontario: Broadview Press, 2002), 446–50.

11. Isobel Armstrong, *Victorian Poetry: Poetry, Poetics and Politics* (London: Routledge, 1993), 336.

12. For a brief but solid introduction to the subject of feeling in this period, see Walter Jackson Bate, 'The Premise of Feeling', in *From Classic to Romantic: Premises of Taste in Eighteenth-Century England* (New York: Harper and Brothers, 1961), 129–59.

13. William Wordsworth, 'Preface to *Lyrical Ballads, with Pastoral and Other Poems*' (1802), in *William Wordsworth: The Poems*, ed. John O. Hayden, 2 vols (London: Penguin, 1977), vol. 1, 867–96 (869–71).

14. See Lionel Trilling, 'The Immortality Ode', in *English Romantic Poets: Modern Essays in Criticism*, ed. M. H. Abrams (Oxford: Oxford University Press, 1975), 149–69 (152).

15. G. Kim Blank, *Wordsworth and Feeling: The Poetry of an Adult Child* (London: Associated University Presses, 1995), 29.

16. William Wordsworth, 'When, to the attractions of the busy world' (1805), in *Poems on the Naming of Places*, ll. 75, 80–83.

17. Dora Greenwell, 'An Inquiry: As to how far the spirit of poetry is alien, and how far friendly, to that of Christianity', *Liber Humanitatis: A Series of Essays on Various Aspects of Spiritual and Social Life* (London: Daldy, Isbister and Co., 1875), 118–44.

18. Greenwell, 'An Inquiry', 125.

19. The period's fascination with women's poetry extended across the Atlantic; see Caroline May, *The American Female Poets* (1848) and *Pearls from the American Female Poets* (1869); Rufus Wilmot Griswold, *The Female Poets of America* (1849); Thomas Buchanan's

The Female Poets of America (1852); and Henry Coppée, *A Gallery of Distinguished English and American Female Poets* (1860).

20. H. N. Coleridge, 'Modern English Poetesses', *Quarterly Review*, 66 (1840), 374–418 (374–5). Notably, John Gibson Lockhart, cited below, was the editor and overseer of the *Quarterly Review* at the time this article was published.
21. John Gibson Lockhart, 'On the Cockney School of Poetry', *Blackwood's Edinburgh Magazine*, 2 (1817), 38–41.
22. See Samuel Taylor Coleridge, *Table Talk* (1836), ed. Carl Woodring, 2 vols (Princeton: Princeton University Press, 1990), 1 September 1832, vol. 2, 190. For an informative discussion of this, see Susan J. Wolfson, 'Gendering the Soul', in Paula R. Feldman and Theresa M. Kelley (ed.), *Romantic Women Writers: Voices and Countervoices* (Hanover and London: University Press of New England, 1995), 33–68.
23. William Michael Rossetti, 'Prefatory Notice', in *The Poetical Works of Mrs Felicia Hemans*, ed. with a Critical Memoir by William Michael Rossetti (London: E. Moxon, Son, & Company, 1873), xi–xxviii (xxvii).
24. William Godwin, *Memoirs of the Author of a Vindication of the Rights of Woman*, 2nd edn (London: Joseph Johnson, 1798), in *Romantic Period Writings 1798–1832: An Anthology*, ed. Zachary Leader and Ian Haywood (London: Routledge, 1998), 156–8 (157).
25. Countess of Blessington, 'Stock in Trade of Modern Poetesses', in Frederic Mansel Reynolds (ed.), *The Keepsake* (London: Longman, Rees, Orme, Brown, Green and Longman, 1833), 208–9 (ll. 25–6).
26. Felicia Hemans, letter to anon., 27 August 1832, in Henry F. Chorley, *Memorials of Mrs Hemans*, with illustrations of her literary character from her private correspondence, 2 vols (London: Saunders and Otley, 1836), 280.
27. Mary Robinson, 'Account of Sappho', in *Sappho and Phaon* (1796; Otley: Woodstock Books, 2000), 21–30.
28. Chorley, *Memorials*, vol. 1, 304.
29. De Staël, *Corinne*, 45.
30. Elizabeth Barrett Browning, Preface, *Poems* (1844), in Daniel Karlin (ed.), *The Penguin Book of Victorian Verse* (Harmondsworth: Penguin, 1998), lv.
31. Karlin, ed., *Victorian Verse*.
32. Anne K. Mellor, *Mothers of the Nation: Women's Political Writing in England 1780–1830* (Indianapolis: Indiana University Press, 2000), 70. For a potted version of the argument, see Mellor's 'The Female Poet and the Poetess: Two Traditions of British Women's Poetry, 1780–1830', *Studies in Romanticism*, 36 (1997), 261–76.

33. Virginia Blain, 'Women Poets and the Challenge of Genre', in Joanne Shattock (ed.), *Women and Literature in Britain, 1800–1900* (Cambridge: Cambridge University Press, 2001), 162–88. Blain insightfully compares Karlin's surmises to 'early (male) reactions to women as undergraduates in the universities, where they were constantly ridiculed for taking their studies too seriously' (170).

34. Isobel Armstrong, 'The Gush of the Feminine: How Can we Read Women's Poetry of the Romantic Period?', in Feldman and Kelley (ed.), *Romantic Women Writers*, 13–32 (15).

35. See Catherine Maxwell, *The Female Sublime from Milton to Swinburne: Bearing Blindness* (Manchester: Manchester University Press, 2001); and also Douglas Bush, *Mythology and the Romantic Tradition in English Poetry* (Cambridge, MA: Harvard University Press, 1987).

36. Percy Bysshe Shelley, 'Defence of Poetry' (1821), Donald H. Reiman and Sharon B. Powers (ed.), *Shelley's Poetry and Prose* (London and New York: Norton, 1977), 480–508 (486).

37. John Stuart Mill, 'What is Poetry' (1833), in F. Parvin Sharples (ed.), *Essays on Poetry* (Columbia: University of South Carolina Press, 1976), 3–22.

38. The verse reads: 'What strain? – oh! not the nightingale's when showering/ Her own heart's life drops on the burning lay, / She stirs the young woods in the days of flowering,/ And pours her strength, but not her grief away'; the epigraph to 'St Cecilia' is from Wordsworth's 'How rich that forehead's calm expanse!'

39. Compare Theodor Adorno's argument in 'On Lyric Poetry and Society' (1957), wherein he argues that the poetic work is 'opposed to society' and therefore able to resist 'anything heteronomous', in *Notes to Literature*, ed. Rolf Tiedemann, trans. Shirley Weber Nicholson, 2 vols (New York: Columbia University Press, 1991), vol. 1, 37–54.

40. For an engaging study of the lyric as a communitarian genre produced by secular, political movements, see Anne Janowitz, *Lyric and Labour in the Romantic Tradition* (Cambridge: Cambridge University Press, 1998).

41. Felicia Hemans, Preface, *Scenes and Hymns of Life, with Other Religious Poems* (Edinburgh: William Blackwood; London: T. Cadell, 1834), vii.

42. The phrase 'healing relief' in this context is Frederick W. Robertson's, in *Lectures and Addresses on Literary and Social Topics* (London: Smith, Elder and Co., 1861), 100.

43. The 'anxiety of influence' argument is forwarded by Harold Bloom, *The Anxiety of Influence: A Theory of Poetry* (Oxford: Oxford

University Press, 1997); on the specific question of women within this formulation, see Annette Kolody, 'The Influence of Anxiety: Prolegomena to a Study of the Production of Poetry by Women', in Marie Harris and Kathleen Aguero (ed.), *A Gift of Tongues: Critical Challenges in Contemporary American Poetry* (Athens: University of Georgia Press, 1988), 112–41.

44. On the theological and poetical implications of reserve, see Sheridan Gilley, 'John Keble and the Victorian Churching of Romanticism', in J. R. Watson (ed.), *An Infinite Complexity: Essays in Romanticism* (Edinburgh: Edinburgh University Press for the University of Durham, 1983), 226–39; and Emma Mason, 'Christina Rossetti and the Doctrine of Reserve', *Journal of Victorian Culture*, 7:2 (2002), 196–219.

45. John Keble, *Lectures on Poetry 1832–41*, trans. Edward Kershaw Francis, 2 vols (Oxford: Clarendon Press, 1912), vol. 1, 21. Keble delivered his *Lectures on Poetry* in Latin in his capacity as Oxford Professor of Poetry between 1832 and 1841; they were published in Latin in 1844 and translated into English in 1912.

46. Keble, *Lectures on Poetry*, vol. 1, 22, 68.

47. Keble, *Lectures on Poetry*, vol. 1, 77.

48. The full dedication reads: 'To William Wordsworth: True Philosopher and Inspired Poet who by the Special Gift and Calling of Almighty God whether he sang of Man or of Nature Failed not to Lift up Men's Hearts to Holy Things nor ever ceased to Champion the Cause of the Poor and Simple and so in Perilous Times was Raised up to be a Chief Minister not only of Sweetest Poetry but also of High and Sacred Truth This Tribute, Slight though it may be, is offered by one of the Multitude who feel ever indebted for the Immortal Treasure of his Splendid Poems in Testimony of Respect, Affection and Gratitude' (Keble, *Lectures on Poetry*, vol. 1, 8).

49. On Wordsworth's privileging of belief over doctrine, see Mark Canuel, *Religion, Toleration and British Writing 1790–1830* (Cambridge: Cambridge University Press, 2002), notably chapter 5, 'Wordsworth and the "frame of social being" ', 161–204.

50. See, for example, Richard Cronin's useful commentary on the inadequacy of modern criticism to deal with Hemans, in *Romantic Victorians: English Literature 1824–1840* (Basingstoke: Palgrave, 2002), 67ff.

51. See J. Julian's *A Dictionary of Hymnology* (1892); A. H. Miles, ed., *The Poets and the Poetry of the Nineteenth Century* (London: 1905–7); William B. Thesing (ed.), *Late Nineteenth and Early Twentieth Century British Women Poets* (London and Detroit: Gale Research, 2001); and most Victorian editions of *Hymns Ancient and Modern*.

52. George Gilfillan, 'Mrs Hemans', *A Second Gallery of Literary Portraits* (Edinburgh: James Hogg, 1850), 256–68 (267).

53. John Keble, 'Sacred Poetry' *Quarterly Review*, 32 (1825), 211–32; and John Henry Newman, 'Poetry: With Reference to Aristotle's Poetics', *London Review*, 1:1 (1829), 153–71, both reprinted in *Poets, Poems and Poetics in Nineteenth-Century Literary Journals*, ed. John Valdimir-Price, (London: Foundations of Literary Theory: The Nineteenth Century in Six Volumes, Routledge-Thoemmes Press, 1995), 211–32 and 153–71.

54. Thomas Carlyle, 'The Hero as Poet' (1841), in *On Heroes, Hero-Worship and the Heroic in History*, *The Works of Thomas Carlyle*, 30 vols (London: Chapman and Hall, 1896–99), V, 80–81.

55. Cynthia Scheinberg, 'Victorian Poetry and Religious Diversity', in Joseph Bristow (ed.), *The Cambridge Companion to Victorian Poetry* (Cambridge: Cambridge University Press, 2000), 159–79.

56. On Roman Catholicism, see Denis Gwynn, *The Second Spring 1818–1852: A Study of the Catholic Revival in England* (London: Burns, Oates, 1942); on the Oxford Movement, see George Herring, *What was the Oxford Movement* (London: Continuum, 2002); on Judaism, see Cynthia Scheinberg, *Women's Poetry and Religion in Victorian England: Jewish Identity and Christian Culture* (Cambridge: Cambridge University Press, 2002); and on eastern religions, see Paul Davies, *Romanticism and Esoteric Tradition: Studies in Imagination* (New York: Lindisfarne, 1998).

57. Matthew Arnold, 'The Study of Poetry', introduction to T. H. Ward's anthology, *The English Poets: Ben Jonson to Dryden* (London: Macmillan, 1880), in Dorothy Mermin and Herbert F. Tucker (ed.), *Victorian Literature 1830–1900* (London: Harcourt, 2002), 757–62 (757).

58. Elizabeth McChesney, personal conversation with Constance L. Maynard, in Maynard, *Dora Greenwell: A Prophet for our own Times on the Battleground of our Faith* (London: H. R. Allenson, 1926), 138.

59. See my discussion of affection in chapter 1.

60. Friedrich Schiller, 'On Simple and Sentimental Poetry' (1795–96), in *Essays Aesthetical and Philosophical* (London: George Bell and Sons, 1900), 262–332 (300).

61. Samuel Taylor Coleridge, letter to Robert Southey, 3 November 1794, in Earl Leslie Griggs (ed.), *Collected Letters of Samuel Taylor Coleridge*, 6 vols (Oxford: Clarendon Press, 1956–1971), vol. 1, 122; and see Michael John Kooy, *Coleridge, Schiller and Aesthetic Education* (Basingstoke: Palgrave, 2002), 9, 17.

62. Friedrich Schiller, *The Poems of Schiller*, trans. E. A. Bowring (London: George Bell, 1882), 272.

63. E. H. Gombrich, 'The Symbol of the Veil: Psychological Reflections on Schiller's Poetry', in Peregrine Horden, *Freud and the Humanities* (New York: St Martin's Press, 1985), 75–109 (90).

64. Felicia Hemans, letter to anon. (a cousin), 1830, in Chorley, *Memorials*, vol. 2, 139–40, 146; see also Hemans's essay, 'German Studies: Scenes and Passages from the "Tasso" of Goethe', *New Monthly Magazine*, 40 (January 1834), 1–8.

65. See Walter Benjamin, *Der Begriff der Kunstkritik in der deutschen Romantik, or The Concept of Art Criticism in German Romanticism* (1920), in Marcus Bullock and Michael W. Jennings (ed.), *Walter Benjamin: Selected Writings Volume One: 1913–1926* (Harvard: Harvard University Press, 1996), 116–200.

66. John Dennis, *The Grounds of Criticism in Poetry* (1704), in Edward Niles Hooker (ed.), *The Critical Works of John Dennis, Volume One 1692–1711*, 2 vols (Baltimore: Johns Hopkins Press, 1939), 325–73 (340); see also *The Advancement and Reformation of Modern Poetry* (1701) and *A Large Account of the Taste in Poetry* (1702), both in Hooker, *Critical Works*, 197–278 and 279–95.

67. See Jon Mee, *Romanticism, Enthusiasm, and Regulation: Poetics and the Policing of Culture in the Romantic Period* (Oxford: Oxford University Press, 2003).

68. See Kirstie Blair, 'Proved on the Pulses: the Heart in Nineteenth-Century Poetry, 1830–1860' (D.Phil diss., Oxford University, 2003); and see how christianity and nervous disorder explosively, and compellingly, merge in Daniel Paul Schreber's turn of the century *Memoirs of my Nervous Illness*, trans. Ida Macalpine and Richard A. Hunter (New York: New York Review of Books, 2000).

69. See, for example, Emily St Aubert's succession of fainting fits remedied only by her appeals to reason in *The Mysteries of Udolpho*, ed. Bonamy Dobrée, intro. Terry Castle (1794; Oxford: Oxford University Press, 1998).

CHAPTER 2. FELICIA HEMANS

1. Henry F. Chorley, *Memorials of Mrs Hemans*, with illustrations of her literary character from her private correspondence, 2 vols (London: Saunders and Otley, 1836), vol. 1, 200.

2. Mackenzie Bell, 'Felicia Dorothea Hemans 1793–1835', in Alfred H. Miles (ed.), *The Poets and the Poetry of the Nineteenth-Century: Joanna Baillie to Jean Ingelow* (London: George Routledge and Sons, 1891), 53–8 (53); Frederic Rowton, 'Felicia Hemans', *The Female Poets of Great Britain, chronologically arranged with copious selections*

and critical remarks (London: Longman, Brown, Green and Longmans, 1848), 407–15 (407).

3. Eric S. Robertson, *English Poetesses: A Series of Critical Biographies with Illustrative Extracts* (London: Cassell and Co. Ltd, 1883), 185, 294; William Michael Rossetti, Prefatory Notice, *The Poetical Works of Mrs Felicia Hemans*, ed. with a Critical Memoir by William Michael Rossetti (London: E. Moxon, Son, & Company, 1873), xi–xxviii (xxv); Arthur Symons, *The Romantic Movement in English Poetry* (London: Archibald Constable and Co. Ltd., 1909).

4. Gary Kelly (ed.), *Felicia Hemans: Selected Poems, Prose and Letters* (Ontario: Broadview Press, 2002), 29.

5. Symons, *Romantic Movement*, 295.

6. Robertson, *English Poetesses*, 183; Rowton, 'Felicia Hemans', 409.

7. Janet E. Courtney, *The Adventurous Thirties: A Chapter in the Women's Movement* (London: Oxford University Press, 1933), 31.

8. See Jason Rudy, 'Forms of Passion: Victorian Poetry at the Boundaries of Sensibility' (PhD diss., Rutgers University, 2003).

9. Marlon B. Ross, Foreword, in Nanora Sweet and Julie Melnyk (ed.), *Felicia Hemans: Reimagining Poetry in the Nineteenth Century* (Basingstoke: Palgrave, 2001), x–xxvi (xviii).

10. Charles William Sutton, 'Felicia Dorothea Hemans 1793–1835', in *Dictionary of National Biography* (Oxford: Oxford University Press, 1995).

11. See Pierre Bourdieu, *Distinction: A Social Critique of the Judgement of Taste*, trans. Richard Nice (Cambridge, MA: Harvard University Press, 1984).

12. Tricia Lootens, 'Hemans and Home: Victorianism, Feminine "Internal Enemies," and the Domestication of National Identity', *PMLA*, 109 (1994), 238–53 (239, 249).

13. See T. S. Eliot, 'The Metaphysical Poets' (1921), *Selected Essays* (London: Faber and Faber, 1999), 281–91.

14. Felicia Hemans, letter to anon., *c.*1828, in Chorley, *Memorials*, vol. 1, 212.

15. Harriet Hughes, *The Works of Mrs Hemans with a Memoir by Her Sister*, 7 vols (Edinburgh: William Blackwood and Sons, 1839), vol. 1, 4.

16. Chorley, *Memorials*, vol. 1, 122.

17. Felicia Hemans, letter to her aunt, 19 December 1808, in Chorley, *Memorials*, vol. 1, 29.

18. Hemans's sons were all attracted abroad, influenced by their mother's cosmopolitan outlook: Arthur went to Rome, where he died in 1837; Claude and Henry William both spent much of their lives in America; Charles Isidore moved to Roman Campagna; and George became a civil engineer in Ireland.

19. Courtney, *Adventurous Thirties*, 24.
20. Kelly, *Selected*, 66.
21. L. B. Walford, *Twelve English Authoresses* (London: Longmans, Green and Co., 1892), 94.
22. John Hollander, *The Work of Poetry* (New York: Columbia University Press, 1997), 68, 71, 73. Hollander notes that the Latin word *focus*, meaning 'hearth' or 'fireplace', even served as a metonym for the 'household' or home, paralleling the Greek word *nostos*, meaning a return to the home and 'on loan to English' in the word 'nostalgia'.
23. Chorley, *Memorials*, vol. 1, 174.
24. Rowton, 'Felicia Hemans' 408.
25. William Wordsworth, comment made to Isabella Fenwick, in *The Fenwick Notes of William Wordsworth*, ed. Jared Curtis (London: Bristol Classical Press, 1993), 60.
26. Felicia Hemans, letter to anon., 25 June 1830, in Chorley, *Memorials*, vol. 2, 119.
27. Kelly, *Selected*, 20.
28. Marlon B. Ross, *The Contours of Masculine Desire: Romanticism and the Rise of Women's Poetry* (Oxford: Oxford University Press, 1989), 292.
29. Kelly, *Selected*, 15. See also Gary Kelly's 'Death and the Matron: Felicia Hemans, Romantic Dearth, and the Founding of the Modern Liberal State', in Sweet and Melnyk (ed.), *Felicia Hemans*, 196–211.
30. On Gladstone, see Kelly, *Selected*, 69; Robert Peel to Felicia Hemans, 7 February 1835, British Library Additional MS 40413 f.291; also in Kelly, *Selected*, 444.
31. Hughes, *Works of Mrs Hemans*, vol. 1, 272–3. Hughes is referring to Hemans's article 'German Studies: Scenes and Passages from the "Tasso" of Goethe', *New Monthly Magazine*, 40 (January 1834), 1–8.
32. Hemans, 'German Studies', 2.
33. Felicia Hemans, letter to anon., 31 March 1831, in Chorley, *Memorials*, vol. 2, 192.
34. William Hazlitt, *Edinburgh Review*, 28 (August 1817), in Douglas Lane Patey, ' "Aesthetics" and the Rise of Lyric in the Eighteenth Century', *Studies in English Literature*, 33 (1993), 587–608 (601).
35. Lane Patey, 'Rise of the Lyric', 602–3. See his discussion of Dugald Stewart's *Elements of the Philosophy of the Human Mind* (1792–1827), which produces, 'in contiguous chapters on "The Poet" and "The Sexes," nearly identical characterizations of (1) women, (2) children, and (3) poets' (p. 603).

36. Edward Young, *Conjectures on Original Composition* (1759), in *The Complete Works, Poetry and Prose*, 2 vols (London, 1854), vol. 2, 43.

37. Paula Feldman, 'The Poet and the Profits: Felicia Hemans and the Literary Marketplace', *Keats–Shelley Journal*, 46 (1997), 148–76.

38. Barbara Hardy, *The Advantage of Lyric: Essays on Feeling in Poetry* (London: Athlone Press, 1977), 1.

39. Hardy, *Advantage of Lyric*, 12.

40. August Wilhelm von Schlegel, *Lectures on Dramatic Art and Literature 1809–1811*, Lecture xxii, in Walter Jackson Bate, *From Classic to Romantic: Premises of Taste in Eighteenth-Century England* (New York: Harper and Brothers, 1946), 131.

41. Chorley, *Memorials*, vol. 1, 110, 199.

42. Theodor Adorno and Max Horkheimer, *Dialectic of Enlightenment* (1943), trans. John Cumming (New York: Continuum, 1994), 3.

43. Maria Jane Jewsbury, 'The History of a Nonchalant', *The Three Histories* (London: Frederick Westley and A. H. Davies, 1830), 193–256, (232); see the discussion of Jewsbury's portrayal of Hemans in the *Histories* below.

44. *Edinburgh Monthly Review*, 2 (August 1819), 194–209, in Kelly, *Felicia Hemans*, 446–50.

45. Lootens, 'Hemans and Home', 239.

46. In addition to the nation poems discussed here, see also Hemans's *Tales, and Historic Scenes* (1819); *A Selection of Welsh Airs* (1822); and *National Lyrics, and Songs for Music* (1834).

47. Stephen C. Behrendt, ' "A few harmless Numbers": British women poets and the climate of war, 1793–1815', in Philip Shaw (ed.), *Romantic Wars: Studies in Culture and Conflict, 1793–1822* (Hampshire: Ashgate, 2000), 13–36 (15).

48. Isobel Armstrong, 'Felicia Hemans' "The Image in Lava" ', in Sweet and Melnyk (ed.), *Felicia Hemans*, 212–30 (220).

49. See, for example, *The Restoration of the Works of Art to Italy: A Poem* (1816), ll. 10ff, 81, 87; and *Modern Greece: A Poem* (1817), stanza XXXVIII.

50. The sonneteers translated from were Vincenzo da Filicaja, Carlo Maria Maggi, Alessandro Marchetti, Alessandro Pegolotti and Francesco Maria de Conti, see Felicia Hemans, Preface, *Patriotic Effusions of the Italian Poets* (1821), in Susan J. Wolfson, *Felicia Hemans: Selected Poems, Letters, Reception Materials* (Princeton and Oxford: Princeton University Press, 2000), 171.

51. Felicia Browne to her mother's sister, 19 December 1808, in Chorley, *Memorials*, vol. 1, 30–33.

52. Chorley, *Memorials*, vol. 1, 89–90.

53. Edmund Burke, *Reflections on the Revolution in France*, ed. L. G. Mitchell (1790; Oxford: Clarendon Press, 1989), 126.
54. Susan J. Wolfson and Elizabeth Fay, Introduction, in Felicia Hemans, *The Siege of Valencia: A Parallel Text Edition: The Manuscript and the Publication of 1823* (Ontario: Broadview, 2002), 7–28 (27).
55. David Rothstein, 'Forming the Chivalric Subject: Felicia Hemans and the Cultural Uses of History, Memory and Nostalgia', *Victorian Literature and Culture*, 27:2 (1999), 49–68.
56. Madame de Staël, *A Treatise on the Influence of the Passions upon the Happiness of Individuals and of Nations* (London: George Cawthorn, 1798), 252.
57. De Staël, *Treatise*, 248, 257.
58. Richard Cronin, *Romantic Victorians: English Literature 1824–1840* (Basingstoke: Palgrave, 2002), 69.
59. Angela Leighton, *Victorian Women Poets: Writing Against the Heart* (London and New York: Harvester Wheatsheaf, 1992), 17.
60. See Stephen C. Behrendt, ' "Certainly not a Female Pen": Felicia Hemans' Early Public Reception', in Sweet and Melnyk (ed.), *Felicia Hemans*, 95–114.
61. Susan J. Wolfson, ' "Domestic Affections" and "the spear of Minerva": Felicia Hemans and the Dilemma of Gender', in Carol Shiner Wilson and Joel Haefner, *Re-visioning Romanticism: British Women Writers 1776–1837* (Philadelphia: University of Pennsylvania Press, 1994), 128–66 (130).
62. Hughes, *Works of Mrs Hemans*, vol. 1, 140; Rossetti, Preface, xxvii; Symons, *Romantic Movement*, 294; and Courtney, *Adventurous Thirties*, 31.
63. Rowton, *Female Poets*, 407.
64. Rose Lawrence, *The Last Autumn at a Favourite Residence with other poems; and Recollections of Mrs Hemans* (London: John Murray, 1836), 288.
65. See Rossetti, Prefatory Notice, xxvii: 'One might sum up the weak points in Mrs Hemans' poetry by saying that it is not only "feminine" poetry (which under the circumstances can be no imputation, rather an ecomium) but also "female" poetry: besides exhibiting the fineness and charm of womanhood, it has the monotone of mere sex.'
66. George Gordon Byron, *Byron's Letters and Journals*, ed. Leslie A. Marchand, 12 vols (Cambridge, MA: Harvard University Press, 1973–82), vol. 7, 183; vol. 7, 158.
67. Jewsbury, 'The History of a Nonchalant', 231.
68. Hughes, *Works of Mrs Hemans*, vol. 1, 131.

69. Susan J. Wolfson, 'Hemans and the Romance of Byron', in Sweet and Melnyk (ed.), *Felicia Hemans*, 155–80 (170).
70. Misquoted translation from de Staël's *Oeuvres complètes* (Paris, 1820), vol. 3, 107–8, in Kelly, *Selected*, 355.
71. Chorley, *Memorials*, vol. 1, 96–7.
72. See Julie D. Prandi, *Spirited Women Heroes: Major Female Characters in the Dramas of Goethe, Schiller and Kleist* (New York: Peter Lang, 1983).
73. Hemans's second epigraph, 'Das ist das Los des Schönen auf der Erde!' ('That is the lot of the splendid in the world'), is from Thekla's last monologue in Act 4, scene 12 of the third part of Schiller's trilogy *Wallenstein* (1798–9); see Wolfson, *Felicia Hemans*, 329.
74. Virginia Jackson and Yopie Prins, 'Lyrical Studies', *Victorian Literature and Culture*, 27:2 (1999), 521–30 (524–5).
75. Kelly, *Selected*, 29.
76. Chorley, *Memorials*, vol. 1, 216.
77. Anthony Ashley Cooper, Earl of Shaftesbury, *Characteristics of Men, Manners, Opinions, Times*, ed. John M. Robertson (1711; Indianapolis: Bobbs-Merrill, 1964); and Adam Smith, *Theory of Moral Sentiments*, ed. D. D. Raphael and A. L. MacFie (1759; Oxford: Clarendon, 1976).
78. William Fenner, *A Treatise of the Affections; or, the Soules Pulse*, 2nd edn (London: 1642), 6.
79. Francis Hutcheson, *An Essay on the Nature and Conduct of the Passions and Affections with Illustrations on the Moral Sense*, 3rd edn (1742), a facsimile reproduction with an introduction by Paul McReynolds (Gainesville, Florida: Scholars' Facsimiles and Reprints, 1969), 63.
80. Isaac Watts, *The Doctrines of the Passions Explained and Improved, Or, A Brief and Comprehensive Scheme of the Natural Affections of Mankind, Attempted in a Plain and Easy Method, With an Account of their Names, Nature, Appearances, Effects and different Uses in Human Life to which are subjoined Moral and Divine Rules for the Regulation or Government of them*, 5th edn (London: J. Buckland and T. Longman, 1770), 2, 36; and Isaac Watts, *An Humble Attempt*, in *The Works of the Reverend Isaac Watts, D. D.*, ed. E. Parsons, 7 vols (Leeds, 1800), vol. 4, 31; and *The Improvement of the Mind*, pt 1, *Works*, vol. 6, 258, in Isabel Rivers, *Reason, Grace and Sentiment: A Study of the Language of Religion and Ethics in England 1660–1780*, 2 vols (Cambridge: Cambridge University Press), vol. 1, 175.
81. Isaac Watts, 'A Rational Defence of the Gospel', *Works*, vol. 1, 192, in Rivers, *Reason, Grace and Sentiment*, vol. 1, 187.
82. *Edinburgh Monthly Review*, 3 (April, 1820), 375.

83. *Quarterly Review* (October, 1821), 130–37.
84. Charles Eliot Norton was Professor of Modern Languages at Harvard in the late nineteenth century.
85. Two further small volumes of religious verse appeared during the same period, *Hymns on the Works of Nature* (1833) and *Hymns for Childhood* (1834).
86. Hughes, *Works of Mrs Hemans*, vol. 1, 28–9.
87. As Hemans noted: 'I strive [...] to turn, with even deeper and more unswerving love, to the holy "spirit-land", and guard it with more and more of watchful care, from the intrusion of all that is heartless and worldly. I find Milton, and Wordsworth, and Channing, my ministering angels in this resolve', Felicia Hemans, letter to anon., Dawson Street, 17 March 1833 in Chorley, *Memorials*, vol. 2, 289.
88. Nanora Sweet, 'Hemans, Heber, and Superstition and Revelation', in 'Romantic Passions', ed. Elizabeth Fay, Romantic Circles Praxis Series, April 1998, http://www.rc.umd.edu/praxis/
89. Felicia Hemans, letter to William Wordsworth, n.d. but before April 1834, in Wolfson, *Felicia Hemans*, 517; and Chorley, *Memorials*, vol. 2, 88.
90. Hughes, *Works of Mrs Hemans*, vol. 1, 38.
91. Chorley, *Memorials*, vol. 2, 122.
92. Chorley, *Memorials*, vol. 2, 71.
93. Felicia Hemans, Preface, *Scenes and Hymns of Life, with Other Religious Poems* (Edinburgh: William Blackwood; London: T. Cadell, 1834), vii.
94. Hughes, *Works of Mrs Hemans*, vol. 1, 255.
95. Felicia Hemans, letter to Rose Lawrence, 10 February 1835, in Kelly, *Selected*, 445.
96. Chorley, *Memorials*, vol. 2, 343.
97. The phrase 'Victorian literary monument' is Tricia Lootens' in *Lost Saints: Silence, Gender and Victorian Literary Canonisation* (Charlottesville and London: University Press of Virginia, 1996), 67. Hemans was buried in St Anne's Church, Dawson Street, Dublin, and a memorial tablet to her lies in St Asaph's Cathedral, in the Welsh Vale of Clwyd.
98. Mary Carpenter, 'On the Death of Mrs Hemans', *Voices of the Spirit and Spirit Pictures* (1877), in Kelly, *Selected*, 80.

CHAPTER 3. DORA GREENWELL

1. Dora Greenwell, letter to William Knight, 15 August 1863, in William Dorling, *Memoirs of Dora Greenwell* (London: James

Clarke and Co., 1885), 75. Leigh Hunt (1784–1859) was a leading Romantic essayist, critic and poet; he founded the influential *Examiner* in 1808, and was one of John Gibson Lockhart's victims in his attack on the 'Cockney school' of poetics.

2. Dora Greenwell, *Two Friends* (Boston: Ticknor and Fields, 1863), 49.
3. Dora Greenwell, 'Stray Leaves', in Dorling, *Memoirs*, 20–21. 'Stray Leaves' is not in print, the only existing copy, the original, held in the Janet Camp Troxell Collection of Rossetti Manuscripts in the Firestone Library, Princeton University; for more on the manuscript, see Janet Gray, 'Dora Greenwell's Commonplace Book', *Princeton University Library Chronicle*, 57:1 (1995), 47–74.
4. Dora Greenwell, *Camera Obscura* (London: Daldy, Isbister and Co., 1876), 68, quoting Elizabeth Barrett Browning, *The Greek Christian Poets and the English Poets* (London: Chapman and Hall, 1863), although Greenwell probably saw the quotation in George Bernard Shaw, 'Elizabeth Barrett Browning', *Cornhill Magazine* (1874), 471–90 (472).
5. Constance L. Maynard, *Dora Greenwell: A Prophet for our own Times on the Battleground of our Faith* (London: H. R. Allenson, 1926), 9.
6. In Angela Leighton and Margaret Reynolds (ed.), *Victorian Women Poets: An Anthology* (Oxford: Blackwell, 1995), 276.
7. Maynard, *Dora Greenwell*, 200.
8. Greenwell, 'An Inquiry: As to how far the spirit of poetry is alien, and how far friendly, to that of Christianity', *Liber Humanitatis: A Series of Essays on Various Aspects of Spiritual and Social Life* (London: Daldy, Isbister and Co., 1875), 118–44 (135).
9. Greenwell, *A Present Heaven: Letters to a Friend* (Edinburgh: Thomas Constable and Co., 1855), 8.
10. Henry Bett, *Dora Greenwell* (London: Epworth Press, 1950), 38–40.
11. Leighton and Reynolds (ed.), *Victorian Women Poets*, 276.
12. Dora Greenwell, letter to Archie Constable, 2 January 1869, in Dorling, *Memoirs*, 64.
13. Dorling, *Memoirs*, 139.
14. The stories were published separately by Strahan and Co in 1868.
15. Dora Greenwell, 'Our Single Women', *Essays* (London and New York: Alexander Strahan, 1866), 1–68 (4).
16. Greenwell, 'Our Single Women', 12, 19.
17. Greenwell, 'Our Single Women', 67, 68.
18. Greenwell, 'Our Single Women', 27.

19. For an introduction to French feminism, see Ann Rosalind Jones, 'Inscribing femininity: French theories of the feminine', in Gayle Greene and Coppélia Kahn, *Making a Difference: Feminist Literary Criticism* (London: Routledge, 1985), 80–112.
20. Also 'Ferdosi', born in about 940 and remembered for writing the Iranian national epic *Shahnameh* or *Book of Kings*.
21. Dorling, *Memoirs*, 160.
22. Dorling, *Memoirs*, 159.
23. Elizabeth McChesney, personal conversation with Maynard, recorded in Maynard, *Dora Greenwell*, 138.
24. See Maynard, *Dora Greenwell*, 143.
25. Dora Greenwell, 'Popular Religious Literature', in *Essays*, 149–207 (154).
26. Greenwell, 'Popular Religious Literature', 155, 161, 167.
27. Greenwell, 'Popular Religious Literature', 167.
28. Greenwell, 'Popular Religious Literature', 158; and see Hannah More, *The Cottage Cook, or, Mrs. Jones's cheap dishes; shewing the way to do much good with little money* (London: J. Marshall, 1797).
29. Greenwell, 'Popular Religious Literature', 153.
30. Greenwell, 'Popular Religious Literature', 188.
31. Greenwell, *A Present Heaven*, 26.
32. Dora Greenwell, letter to William Knight, 4 February 1865, in Dorling, *Memoirs*, 93.
33. On prayer, see also Greenwell's 'Prayer as Will', in Dora Greenwell and P. T. Forsyth, *The Power of Prayer* (London: Hodder and Stoughton, 1910), 1–51.
34. For an enlightening and sympathetic portrait of Knight, see Stephen Gill, *Wordsworth and the Victorians* (Oxford: Clarendon Press, 1998), especially chapter 7.
35. See Dora Greenwell, *Lacordaire* (Edinburgh: Edmonston and Douglas, 1867). It is notable that Greenwell's 300-page biography of the Catholic Lacordaire triumphs in content and style over her sixty-page biography of the American Quaker John Woolman, in whom she seems infinitely less interested; see *John Woolman* (London: F. B. Kitton, 1871).
36. Dora Greenwell, letter to William Knight, 4 February 1865, in Dorling, *Memoirs*, 89.
37. Dora Greenwell, letter to William Knight, 4 February 1865, in Dorling, *Memoirs*, 92.
38. Dora Greenwell, 'Is Romanism a Corruption of Christianity, or is it its Natural Development? Three Letters to a Friend in Answer to an Inquiry so Worded in "The Index" (American Journal), May, 1872', in *Liber Humanitatis*, 173–219 (179).

39. Greenwell, 'Romanism', 192.
40. Greenwell, 'Romanism', 194.
41. Greenwell, 'Romanism', 196; my emphasis.
42. Friedrich Schiller, *On the Aesthetic Education of Man: in a Series of Letters*, ed. and trans. Elizabeth M. Wilkinson and L. A. Willoughby (1795; Oxford: Clarendon Press, 1967), 39–43.
43. Walter Richard Cassels, *Supernatural Religion an Inquiry into the Reality of Divine Revelation*, Popular Edition (London: Watts and Co, 1902), 912.
44. Greenwell, 'Prayer', in *Essays*, 114–48 (114).
45. M. H. Abrams, *Natural Supernaturalism: Tradition and Revolution in Romantic Literature* (London: Norton, 1971), 216; and Friedrich Schiller, *The Philosophical and Aesthetic Letters and Essays*, trans. J. Weiss (London: Chapman, 1845), 59.
46. Greenwell, 'Prayer', 115–16.
47. Greenwell, 'Prayer', 128.
48. Greenwell, 'Prayer', 128.
49. See 'Prayer', 130; and 'On the Connection between the Animal and the Spiritual Nature in Man', *Liber Humanitatis*, 20–46 (23).
50. Greenwell, 'On the Relation between Natural and Supernatural Life', *Liber Humanitatis*, 47–65 (52).
51. Schiller, 'On Simple and Sentimental Poetry' (1795–6), *Essays Aesthetical and Philosophical* (London: George Bell and Sons, 1900), 262–332 (307).
52. Schiller, 'On Simple and Sentimental Poetry', 266.
53. Schiller, 'On Simple and Sentimental Poetry', 289.
54. Schiller, 'On Simple and Sentimental Poetry', 285.
55. Schiller, 'On Simple and Sentimental Poetry', 307; and Greenwell, 'An Inquiry,' 131.
56. Schiller, 'On Simple and Sentimental Poetry', 300.
57. Schiller, 'On the Connection between the Animal and the Spiritual Nature in Man' (1780), *Essays Aesthetical and Philosophical* (London: George Bell and Sons, 1900), 400–35 (400, 402).
58. Schiller, 'On the Connection', 403, 417.
59. Schiller, 'On the Connection', 407.
60. Schiller, 'On the Connection', 422.
61. Greenwell, 'On the Connection', 208.
62. Schiller, 'On the Connection', 427.
63. Greenwell, 'On the Connection', 22. Greenwell cites Robert Burns's 'Epistle to a Young Friend' (1786): 'I waive the quantum o' the sin,/ The hazard of concealing;/ But, Och! it hardens a' within,/ And petrifies the feelin'!' (ll. 45–8).
64. Greenwell, ''Natural and Supernatural Life', 64–5.

65. Greenwell, ''Natural and Supernatural Life', 65.
66. Greenwell, 'Is Romanism a Corruption of Christianity, or is it its Natural Development? *Liber Humanitatis*, 173–219 (196).
67. Greenwell, 'Folk-Lore', *Liber Humanitatis*, 145–72 (171).
68. Greenwell, 'On the Connection', 26.
69. Greenwell, 'On the Connection', 25.
70. Dora Greenwell, letter to William Knight, 8 January 1868, in Dorling, *Memoirs*, 68.
71. Greenwell, *Two Friends*, 46–7.
72. Greenwell, *Two Friends*, 38.
73. Greenwell, *Two Friends*, 49.
74. Greenwell, *Two Friends*, 51.
75. Greenwell, *Two Friends*, 53–4.
76. Greenwell, 'On the Comparative Freedom of the Will', *Liber Humanitatis*, 66–84 (70).
77. Dora Greenwell, *A Basket of Summer Fruit* (London: Daldy, Isbister and Co, 1877), 52.
78. Dora Greenwell, letter to William Knight, 5 April 1866, in Dorling, *Memoirs*, 104.
79. Dora Greenwell, letter to William Knight, 5 April 1866, in Dorling, *Memoirs*, 102.
80. Greenwell, 'On the Dignity of the Human Body: Founded upon an Essay of Mr Goodsir's, so Entitled', in *Liber Humanitatis*, 1–19 (10).
81. Greenwell, *A Basket of Summer Fruit*, 31. Guyon was a seventeenth-century mystic; here, Greenwell is probably thinking of her *Autobiography of Madame Guyon*, trans. Thomas Taylor Allen, 2 vols (London, 1897).
82. Greenwell, 'An Inquiry', 126.
83. Greenwell, *Lacordaire*, 156.
84. Greenwell, 'The Spirit of Poetry', 119.
85. Greenwell, 'The Spirit of Poetry', 122.
86. Greenwell, 'The Spirit of Poetry', 132.
87. Greenwell, 'The Spirit of Poetry', 123.
88. Greenwell, 'The Spirit of Poetry', 123, 125.
89. Greenwell, 'The Spirit of Poetry', 124.
90. Greenwell, 'The Spirit of Poetry', 126–7.
91. Greenwell, 'The Spirit of Poetry', 127.
92. Greenwell, 'The Spirit of Poetry', 127–30.
93. Greenwell, 'The Spirit of Poetry', 131.
94. Dora Greenwell, letter to William Knight, 8 January 1868, in Dorling, *Memoirs*, 71.
95. Greenwell, 'The Spirit of Poetry', 131.

96. Greenwell, 'The Spirit of Poetry', 132.
97. Greenwell, 'The Spirit of Poetry', 136.
98. Greenwell, 'The Spirit of Poetry', 142.
99. Greenwell, 'The Spirit of Poetry', 138.
100. Greenwell, 'The Spirit of Poetry', 139.
101. Greenwell, 'The Spirit of Poetry', 144.
102. Samuel Taylor Coleridge, note recorded by Julius Charles Hare, 'in reference to those who almost deify [Nature], No! Nature is not God; she is the devil in a strait waistcoat', in R. J. White (ed.), *The Collected Works of Samuel Taylor Coleridge: Lay Sermons*, 16 vols (London: Routledge and Kegan Paul, 1972), 71n.6.
103. Bernard Richards, *English Poetry of the Victorian Period 1830–1890* (Essex: Longman, 1988), 88.
104. Greenwell, *Camera Obscura*, 68; and for the source, see Arthur Hugh Clough, 'Recent English Poetry', *North American Review*, July 1853.
105. See, for example, 'The Mower-Maiden', 'The Sleeping Girl', 'The Bride's Wreath', 'The Emigrants Daughter' and 'The Little Sister', in *Stories that Might be True, with Other Poems* (London: William Pickering, 1850).
106. See Swinburne's 'Hymn to Proserpine' (1866) and 'The Garden of Proserpine' (1866).
107. See Bett, *Dora Greenwell*, 17. Greenwell also travelled to Italy in 1842 for health reasons, hoping the warm climate would relieve her.
108. See Isaac Williams, 'Tract 80: On Reserve in Communicating Religious Knowledge (Parts I–III)' and 'Tract 87: On Reserve in Communicating Religious Knowledge (Conclusion: Parts IV–VI)', in *Tracts for the Times by members of the University of Oxford*, 6 vols (London: J. G. & F. Rivington, St Paul's Church Yard and Waterloo Place, Pall Mall; & J. H. Parker, Oxford, 1838).
109. The two collections are almost the same, the latter slightly enhanced by seventeen new poems in the 'Valentines and Songs' part of the book, a second sonnet addressing Elizabeth Barrett Browning added and 'Earlier Poems', chiefly from the 1848 *Poems*, replaced with ten 'Later Poems'.

CHAPTER 4. ADELAIDE ANNE PROCTER

1. Frances Ann Kemble, *Record of a Girlhood*, 3 vols (London: Richard Bentley and Son, 1879), vol. 3, 176; Gill Gregory, *The Life and Work of Adelaide Procter: Poetry, Feminism and Fathers* (Aldershot: Ashgate, 1998), 5.

2. Charles Bruce, *The Book of Noble Englishwomen: Lives Made Illustrious by Heroism, Goodness, and Great Attainments* (London: William P. Nimmo, 1875), 445; and see also Bessie Rayner Belloc (Parkes), *In a Walled Garden* (London: Ward and Downey, 1895).

3. Charles Dickens, Introduction, in Adelaide Anne Procter, *Legends and Lyrics Together with a Chaplet of Verses* (London: George Bell and Sons, 1877), xi–xxxi (xxvii).

4. Margaret Maison, 'Queen Victoria's Favourite Poet', *Listener and BBC Television Review*, 29 April 1965, 636.

5. Margaret Maison, 'Queen Victoria's Favourite Poet', 636.

6. Gregory, *Life and Work*, xii.

7. Isobel Armstrong, *Victorian Poetry: Poetry, Poetics and Politics* (London: Routledge, 1993), 337.

8. On the question of intensifying emotion by retaining it, see Robert C. Soloman, *The Passions: Emotions and the Meaning of Life* (Indianapolis: Hackett Publishing, 1993), 171ff.

9. Adelaide Anne Procter, 'Madame Récamier', *Englishwoman's Journal*, vol. 6 (1860–61), pt 1, pp. 225–36 (p. 227); pt 2, pp. 297–305; pt 3, pp. 373–83.

10. Dickens, Introduction, xiii.

11. Charles Bruce, *Book of Noble Englishwomen*, 450.

12. Belloc, *Walled Garden*, 170.

13. 'Golden-Tressed Adelaide: A Song for a Child', 'To Adelaide'; see also 'To Edith: 1845', in which Adelaide is elevated as a role model for her sister Edith.

14. Barry Cornwall, 'On English Poetry', in *Essays and Tales in Prose*, 2 vols (Boston: Ticknor, Reed and Fields, 1853), vol. 2, 132.

15. Barry Cornwall, 'A Defence of Poetry', in *Essays and Tales in Prose*, vol. 2, 189–90.

16. Barry Cornwall, Preface, *Dramatic Scenes and Other Poems*, 2nd edn (London: C. & J. Ollier, 1820), vii.

17. Dickens, Introduction, xvi.

18. Helen Vendler, *The Odes of John Keats* (London: Belknap Press, 1983), 48.

19. See John Stuart Mill, 'What is Poetry' (1833), in F. Parvin Sharples (ed.), *Essays on Poetry* (Columbia: University of South Carolina Press, 1976).

20. See Gregory, *Life and Work*, 7–8. 'Ministering Angels' was published in Marguerite Power, The Countess of Blessington (ed.), *Heath's Book of Beauty* (London: Longman, Brown, Green, and Longmans, 1843), 38.

21. Adelaide Anne Procter, letter to Bessie Parkes, 22 January *c*.1855, MS, Bessie Rayner Parkes Papers, Girton College, Cambridge, Box VIII, 38.

22. John Henry Newman, ' "Second Spring" Sermon', preached at St Mary's, Oscott, at the first Provincial Synod of Westminster in 1852, in Horton Davies, *Worship and Theology in England: From Watts and Wesley to Martineau 1690–1900* (Michigan: Eerdmans, 1996), 17.
23. Belloc, *Walled Garden*, 165.
24. John Henry Newman, *Lectures on Justification*, 3rd edn (London: Rivingtons, 1874), 371–90.
25. Belloc, *Walled Garden*, 168.
26. Davies, *Worship and Theology*, 34.
27. For her enthusiasm regarding Faber, see her unpublished correspondence with Parkes, in the Bessie Rayner Parkes Papers, Girton College Archive, Cambridge.
28. Adelaide Anne Procter, letter to Richard Monckton-Milnes, 1855, in Gregory, *Life and Work*, 15.
29. Isaac Williams, 'Advertisement', *The Cathedral or the Catholic and Apostolic Church in England* (Oxford: John Henry Parker; London: J. G. and F. Rivington, 1838), v.
30. Adelaide Anne Procter, letter to Bessie Parkes, 21? August 1862, MS, Bessie Rayner Parkes Papers, Girton College, Cambridge, Box VIII, 39.
31. See Susan Stewart, *Poetry and the Fate of the Senses* (London and Chicago: University of Chicago Press, 2002), 309ff.
32. William Blake, *A Vision of the Last Judgement* (1810), in David V. Erdman (ed.), *The Poetry and Prose of William Blake* (New York: Doubleday and Co, 1970), 544–55 (544).
33. In this way, Procter is closer to Faber than the ritualist architect A. W. Pugin, the latter associated with a Gothic Revival in Britain to which Faber was opposed. For Pugin's views, see Augustus Welby Northmore Pugin, *Contrasts: or, A Parallel Between the Noble Edifices of the Fourteenth and Fifteenth Centuries, and Similar Buildings of the Present Day; shewing the Present Decay of Tastes* (London: St Marie's Grange, 1836) and *A Treatise on Chancel Screens and Rood Lofts: Their Antiquity, Use and Symbolic Signification* (London: Charles Dolman, 1851). For more on this subject, see James F. White, *The Cambridge Movement: The Ecclesiologists and the Gothic Revival* (Cambridge: Cambridge University Press, 1962) and Nigel Yates, *Buildings, Faith and Worship: The Liturgical Arrangement of Anglican Churches 1600–1900* (Oxford: Clarendon Press, 1991).
34. F. W. Faber, *The Foot of the Cross: or, the Sorrows of Mary* (London: Thomas Richardson and Son, 1858), 396, 444. It is worth noting that Faber dedicated the study to Lady Georgiana Fullerton, 'in

Affectionate Remembrance of a Season of Darkness, which God consecrated for Himself by a more than Common Sorrow'.

35. Procter even wrote 'Birthday Gifts' specifically to convey the figure of Mary to children.

36. Sigmund Freud, quoted by Maria Bergmann and Martin Bergmann, 'Rembrandt's Self-Portraits', Oscar Sternbach Memorial Lecture, National Psychological Association for Psychoanalysis, New York, 2001.

37. Charles Dickens, 'Sucking Pigs', *Household Words*, 8 November 1851, 145–7; see also Kate Flint, *Dickens* (Brighton: Harvester Press, 1986).

38. Handbill, 27 December 1849, quoted in Anne Lohrli, *Household Words: A Weekly Journal 1850–1859 conducted by Charles Dickens, Table of Contents, List of Contributors and their Contributions based on the Household Words Office Book in the Morris L. Parrish Collection of Victorian Novelists, Princeton University Library* (Toronto: University of Toronto Press, 1973), 3n.2, 4.

39. Charles Dickens, letter to Elizabeth Gaskell, 31 January 1850, in Lohrli, *Household Words*, 4n.9.

40. For a full list of Procter's Christmas number contributions, see Gregory, *Life and Work*, 261–3; also in Lohrli, *Household Words*, 405–6.

41. The following discussion refers to the versions of these poems printed in *Legends and Lyrics*, and the titles used therein. The compositions used in the seasonal extras of *Household Words* were often left without titles, being part of the continuous narrative of the Christmas theme.

42. Gregory, *Life and Work*, 223.

43. Charles Dickens, 'The Holly Tree Inn', *Household Words*, Christmas number, 15 December 1855, 30.

44. Charles Dickens, 'The Wreck of the Golden Mary', *Household Words*, Christmas number, 6 December 1856, 25; published as 'Homeward Bound' in *Legends and Lyrics*; the poem here makes up part of the story 'The Beguilement of the Boats', 13–29.

45. Charles Dickens, 'A House to Let', *Household Words*, Christmas number, 7 December 1858, 22. Gregory refers to the poem as 'Three Evenings in a House' (*Life and Work*, 229ff), whereas it is printed in *Household Words* as 'Three Evenings in the House'; the poem was finally published as 'Three Evenings in a Life' in *Legends and Lyrics*.

46. Dickens, 'House to Let', 22.

47. William Makepeace Thackeray, letter to his daughters, December 1854, in Gordon N. Ray, *The Letters and Private Papers of William*

Makepeace Thackeray, 4 vols (Oxford and London: Oxford University Press, 1945–6), vol. 4, 122; and see Gregory, *Life and Work*, 21n.67. No record of the suitor's name exists.

48. See George Smith, *A Memoir with Some Pages of Autobiography*, ed. Mrs E. Smith (London: Private Circulation, 1902), 98.

49. Procter also published in *All the Year Round*, the *Cornhill Magazine* and *Good Words*.

50. Procter's correspondence with Parkes during 1858–9 are suggestive of this romantic relationship in which she readily couples herself with Hays, signing off letters 'Max & me'; see MS in Bessie Rayner Parkes Papers, Girton College, Cambridge, Box VIII, pp. 45–7.

51. Charlotte Cushman was an American actress and patron to the also American neo-classical sculptor, Harriet Hosmer. Theodosia, Dowager Lady Monson, a friend of Anna Jameson, had assisted the Langham Place circle to find premises for their work; see Pam Hirsch, *Barbara Leigh Smith Bodichon: Feminist, Artist and Rebel* (London: Pimlico, 1999), 187ff; Lisa Merrill, *When Romeo Was a Woman: Charlotte Cushman and Her Circle of Female Spectators* (Ann Arbor: University of Michigan Press, 1999); Julia Markus, *Across an Untried Sea* (New York: Alfred A. Knopf, 2000); and Gregory, *Life and Work*, 25.

52. Adelaide Anne Procter, letter to Bessie Parkes, 17 July 1855, MS, Bessie Rayner Parkes Papers, Girton College, Cambridge, Box VIII, 6.

53. On the Langham Place Group, see Margaret Forster, *Significant Sisters: The Grassroots of Active Feminism 1839–1939* (London: Secker and Warburg, 1984); Candida Ann Lacey (ed.), *Barbara Leigh Smith Bodichon and the Langham Place Group* (London and New York: Routledge, 1987); and Ray Strachey, *The Cause: A Short History of the Women's Movement* (1928; London: Virago, 1978); see also the contemporary documents that emerged from the Group, Jessie Boucherett, *Hints on Self-Help: A Book for Young Women* (London: S. W. Partridge, 1863); Frances Power Cobbe, *Essays on the Pursuits of Women* (London: Emily Faithfull, 1863) and *The Duties of Women: A Course of Lectures* (London and Edinburgh: William and Norgate, 1881); Emily Davies, *Thoughts on Some Questions Relating to Women 1860–1908* (Cambridge: Bowes and Bowes, 1910); Anna Jameson, 'A Letter to Lord John Russell', *English Woman's Journal*, 3 (July 1859), 343–52; Bessie Rayner Parkes, 'The Profession of the Teacher', *English Woman's Journal*, 1 (March 1858), 1–13; Bessie Rayner Parkes, *Essays on Woman's Work* (London, 1865).

54. 'Association for the Employment of Women', *English Woman's Journal*, 4 (September 1859), 54–60 (58–9).
55. Procter, 'Adventures of Your Own Correspondents in Search of Solitude', *English Woman's Journal*, 4 (1859), 34–44, 100–114 (35).
56. Procter, 'Solitude', 35–6.
57. Procter, 'Solitude', 102.
58. Procter, 'Solitude', 37, 108.
59. Procter, 'Solitude', 113.
60. On the potentially severe damage city life inflicts on the emotions, see Georg Simmel, 'The Metropolis and Mental Life', in *The Sociology of Georg Simmel*, trans. Kurt Wolff (New York: Free Press, 1950), 409–24.
61. Procter, 'Madame Récamier', pt 1, 229.
62. Procter, 'Madame Récamier', pt 3, 374.
63. See Elaine Marks, 'Lesbian Intertexuality', in Susan J. Wolfe and Julia Penelope (ed.), *Sexual Practice/Textual Theory: Lesbian Cultural Criticism* (Oxford: Blackwell, 1993), 271–90.
64. Procter, 'Madame Récamier', pt 1, 230–31.
65. Procter, 'Madame Récamier', pt 3, 383.
66. On the entanglements of Hays and the Langham Place Group, see Jane Rendall, ' "A Moral Engine": Feminism, Liberalism and *The English Woman's Journal*', in Jane Rendall (ed.), *Equal or Different: Women's Politics 1800–1914* (Oxford: Basil Blackwell, 1987), 112–38.
67. See Dickens, Introduction, xxiv; and Bruce, *Noble Englishwomen*, 447.
68. From Ralph Waldo Emerson, 'Gifts', in *Essays*, Second Series (London, 1844).
69. Gregory, *Life and Work*, 244.
70. Adelaide Anne Procter, letter to Bessie Parkes, 7 August 1862, MS, Bessie Rayner Parkes Papers, Girton College, Cambridge, VIII, 26.
71. In Hays's defence, she wrote daily letters to Procter from Monson's house and the Procter family finally consented to her taking charge of the flowers for the poet's grave at Kensal Green; see Hirsch, *Barbara Bodichon*, 209, 345n.7.
72. Adelaide Anne Procter, letters to Bessie Parkes, date unknown, 1862 and 28? May 1862, MS, Bessie Rayner Parkes Papers, Girton College, Cambridge, VIII, 24 and 27.
73. *Saturday Review*, 7 January 1860, in Hirsch, *Barbara Bodichon*, 197.
74. Dickens, Introduction, xxix.
75. e e cummings, 'A Poet's Advice to Students', in *e.e. cummings: A Miscellany Revised*, ed. George J. Firmage (New York: October House, 1965), 335.

Select Bibliography

Listed below are the three poets' primary texts and the more essential critical works; all other references can be found in the footnotes to individual chapters. Dates given after texts throughout the book refer to time of publication.

FELICIA HEMANS

Works

England and Spain; or Valour and Patriotism (Liverpool and London: Cadell and Davies, 1808).

Poems (Liverpool and London: Cadell and Davies, 1808).

The Domestic Affections, and Other Poems (London: Cadell and Davies, 1812).

The Restoration of the Works of Art to Italy: A Poem (Oxford: R. Pearson; London: J. Ebers, 1816).

Modern Greece: A Poem (London: John Murray, 1817).

Translations from Camoens, and Other Poets, with Original Poetry (Oxford: J. Parker; London: John Murray, 1818).

Tales, and Historic Scenes, in Verse (London: John Murray, 1819).

The Sceptic; A Poem (London: John Murray, 1820).

Stanzas to the Memory of the Late King (London: John Murray, 1820).

Wallace's Invocation to Bruce (Edinburgh: Blackwood, 1820).

Dartmoor: A Poem (London: The Royal Society of Literature, 1821).

A Selection of Welsh Melodies, with Symphonies and Accompaniments by John Parry, and Characteristic Words By Mrs Hemans (London: J. Power, 1822).

The Siege of Valencia: A Dramatic Poem; The Last Constantine: with Other Poems (London: John Murray, 1823).

The Vespers of Palermo: A Tragedy in Five Acts (London: John Murray, 1823).

The Forest Sanctuary: and Other Poems (London: John Murray, 1825).
Hymns for Childhood (Boston: Hilliard, Gray, Little and Wilkins, 1827).
Records of Woman: with Other Poems (Edinburgh: Blackwood, 1828).
Songs of the Affections, with Other Poems (Edinburgh: Blackwood, 1830).
Hymns on the Works of Nature, for the Use of Children (London: John Mardon, 1833).
National Lyrics, and Songs for Music (Dublin: William Curry Jr. and Co., 1834).
Scenes and Hymns of Life, with Other Religious Poems (Edinburgh: Blackwood, 1834).
Poetical Remains of the Late Mrs Hemans (Edinburgh: Blackwood, 1836).
The Works of Mrs Hemans, 7 vols, ed. Harriet Hughes (Edinburgh and London: Blackwood, 1839).
The Poetical Works of Mrs Felicia Hemans, ed. William Michael Rossetti (London: E. Moxon, Son, & Company, 1873).
Felicia Dorothea Hemans: Tales and Historic Scenes, ed. Donald H. Reiman (London: Garland, 1978).
Felicia Hemans: Selected Poems, Letters, Reception Materials, ed. Susan J. Wolfson (Princeton and Oxford: Princeton University Press, 2000).
Felicia Hemans: Selected Poems, Prose and Letters, ed. Gary Kelly (Ontario: Broadview Press, 2002).
Felicia Hemans: The Siege of Valencia, A Parallel Text Edition: The Manuscript and the Publication of 1823, ed. Susan J. Wolfson and Elizabeth Fay (Ontario: Broadview, 2002).

Critical and Biographical Studies

Behrendt, Stephen C., ' "A Few Harmless Numbers"': British Women Poets and the Climate of War, 1793–1815', in Philip Shaw (ed.), *Romantic Wars: Studies in Culture and Conflict, 1793–1822* (Hampshire: Ashgate, 2000), 13–36.
Bell, Mackenzie, 'Felicia Dorothea Hemans 1793–1835', in Alfred H. Miles (ed.), *The Poets and the Poetry of the Nineteenth Century: Joanna Baillie to Jean Ingelow*, (London: George Routledge and Sons, 1891), 53–8.
Chorley, Henry F., *Memorials of Mrs Hemans*, with illustrations of her literary character from her private correspondence, 2 vols (London: Saunders and Otley, 1836).
Clarke, Norma, *Ambitious Heights: Writing, Friendship, Love: The Jewsbury Sisters, Felicia Hemans and Jane Welsh Carlyle* (London: Routledge, 1990).

Courtney, Janet E., *The Adventurous Thirties: A Chapter in the Women's Movement* (London: Oxford University Press, 1933).

Eubanks, Kevin, 'Minerva's Veil: Hemans, Critics, and the Construction of Gender', *European Romantic Review*, 8 (1997), 341–59.

Feldman, Paula R., 'The Poet and the Profits: Felicia Hemans and the Literary Marketplace', *Keats–Shelley Journal*, 46 (1997), 148–76.

Gilfillan, George, 'Mrs Hemans', *A Second Gallery of Literary Portraits* (Edinburgh: James Hogg, 1850), 256–68.

Harding, Anthony John, 'Felicia Hemans and the Effacement of Woman', in Paula R. Feldman and Theresa M. Kelley (eds), *Romantic Women Writers: Voices and Countervoices* (Hanover and London: University Press of New England, 1995), 138–49.

Jewsbury, Maria Jane, *The Three Histories* (London: Frederick Westley and A. H. Davies, 1830).

Kelly, Gary (ed.), Introduction, *Felicia Hemans: Selected Poems, Prose and Letters* (Ontario: Broadview Press, 2002), 15–85.

Kennedy, Deborah, 'Hemans, Wordsworth and the "Literary Lady" ', *Victorian Poetry*, 33 (1997), 257–86.

Landon, Letitia Elizabeth, 'On the Character of Mrs Hemans' Writings,' *New Monthly Magazine*, 44 (1835), in Jerome McGann and Daniel Riess, *Letitia Elizabeth Landon: Selected Writings* (Ontario: Broadview, 1997), 173–86.

Lawrence, Rose, *The Last Autumn at a Favourite Residence with Other Poems; and Recollections of Mrs Hemans* (London: John Murray, 1836).

Linley, Margaret, 'Sappho's Conversions in Felicia Hemans, Letitia Landon and Christina Rossetti', *Prism(s): Essays in Romanticism*, 4 (1996), 15–42.

Lootens, Tricia, *Lost Saints: Silence, Gender and Victorian Literary Canonisation* (Charlottesville and London: University Press of Virginia, 1996).

Lootens, Tricia, 'Hemans and Home: Victorianism, Feminine 'Internal Enemies,' and the Domestication of National Identity', *PMLA*, 109 (1994), 238–53.

Robertson, Eric S., *English Poetesses: A Series of Critical Biographies with Illustrative Extracts* (London: Cassell and Co. Ltd, 1883).

Ross, Marlon B., *The Contours of Masculine Desire: Romanticism and the Rise of Women's Poetry* (Oxford: Oxford University Press, 1989).

Rossetti, William Michael, Prefatory Notice, *The Poetical Works of Mrs Felicia Hemans* ed. with a Critical Memoir by William Michael Rossetti (London: E. Moxon, Son, & Company, 1873), xi–xxviii.

Rothstein, David, 'Forming the Chivalric Subject: Felicia Hemans and the Cultural Uses of History, Memory and Nostalgia', *Victorian Literature and Culture*, 27:2 (1999), 49–68.

Rowton, Frederic, 'Felicia Hemans', *The Female Poets of Great Britain, Chronologically Arranged with Copious Selections and Critical Remarks* (London: Longman, Brown, Green and Longmans, 1848), 407–15.

Sweet, Nanora, 'Hemans, Heber, and Superstition and Revelation', in *Romantic Passions*, ed. Elizabeth Fay, *Romantic Circles Praxis* series (1998) www.rc.umd.edu/praxis/.

Sweet, Nanora, and Julie Melnyk (eds), *Felicia Hemans: Reimagining Poetry in the Nineteenth Century* (Basingstoke: Palgrave, 2001).

Sweet, Nanora, and Barbara Taylor, *The Sceptic: a Hemans–Byron Dialogue*, Romantic Circles Electronic Edition (2004), www.rc.umd.edu/editions/sceptic/.

Symons, Arthur, *The Romantic Movement in English Poetry* (London: Archibald Constable and Co. Ltd., 1909).

Trinder, Peter, *Mrs Hemans* (Cardiff: University of Wales Press, 1984).

Walford, L. B., *Twelve English Authoresses* (London: Longmans, Green and Co., 1892).

Wolfson, Susan J., Introduction, *Felicia Hemans: Selected Poems, Letters, Reception Materials* (Princeton and Oxford: Princeton University Press, 2000), xiii–xxix.

Wolfson, Susan J., and Elizabeth Fay (eds), Introduction, *Felicia Hemans: The Siege of Valencia, A Parallel Text Edition: The Manuscript and the Publication of 1823* (Ontario: Broadview, 2002), 7–28.

DORA GREENWELL

Works

Poems (London: William Pickering, 1848).

Stories that Might be True, with Other Poems (London: William Pickering, 1850).

A Present Heaven: Letters to a Friend (Edinburgh: Thomas Constable and Co., 1855).

The Patience of Hope (Boston: Ticknor and Fields, 1862).

Two Friends (Boston: Ticknor and Fields, 1862).

Essays (London and New York: Alexander Strahan, 1866).

Lacordaire (Edinburgh: Edmonston and Douglas, 1867).

Carmina Crucis (London: Bell and Daldy, 1869).

Colloquia Crucis, A Sequel to 'Two Friends' (London: Strahan and Co, 1871).

John Woolman (London: F. B. Kitto, 1871).

Songs of Salvation (London: Strahan and Co., 1873).

The Soul's Legend (London: Strahan and Co., 1873).

Liber Humanitatis: A Series of Essays on Various Aspects of Spiritual and Social Life (London: Daldy, Isbister and Co., 1875).

Camera Obscura (London: Daldy, Isbister and Co., 1876).
A Basket of Summer Fruit (London: Daldy, Isbister and Co, 1877).
Poems by Dora Greenwell (Selected), ed. William Dorling (London: Walter Scott, 1889).

Critical and Biographical Studies

Bett, Henry, *Dora Greenwell* (London: Epworth Press, 1950).
Dorling, William, *Memoirs of Dora Greenwell* (London: James Clarke and Co., 1885).
Dorling, William, Introduction, *Poems by Dora Greenwell (Selected)*, ed. William Dorling (London: Walter Scott, 1889), ix–xxii.
Gray, Janet, 'Dora Greenwell's Commonplace Book', *Princeton University Library Chronicle*, 57:1 (1995), 47–74.
Maynard, Constance L., *Dora Greenwell: A Prophet for our own Times on the Battleground of our Faith* (London: H. R. Allenson, 1926).

ADELAIDE ANNE PROCTER

Works

'Hidden Light', *Household Words*, 26:8 (1854).
'Words upon the Waters', *Household Words*, 6:5 (1854).
'Watch Cry: From a German Patois Song', *Household Words*, 22:3 (1856).
Legends and Lyrics, first series (London: Bell and Daldy, 1858).
'Adventures of Your Own Correspondents in Search of Solitude', *English Woman's Journal*, 4 (1859), 34–44, 100–114.
'Letter Reporting on a Visit to a Watch-making Factory in Christchurch, Dorset', *English Woman's Journal*, 4 (1859), 278–9.
Legends and Lyrics, second series (London: Bell and Daldy, 1861).
'Madame Récamier,' *English Woman's Journal*, 6 (1860), 225–36 (1861), 297–305, 373–83.
A Chaplet of Verses (London: Longman, Green, Longman and Roberts, 1862).
Legends and Lyrics Together with a Chaplet of Verses, ed. Charles Dickens (London: George Bell and Sons, 1877).
The Angel's Story (London: George Bell and Sons, 1881)

Critical and Biographical Studies

Belloc, Bessie Rayner, *In a Walled Garden* (London: Ward and Downey, 1895).

Bruce, Charles, *The Book of Noble Englishwomen: Lives Made Illustrious by Heroism, Goodness, and Great Attainments* (London: William P. Nimmo, 1875).

Dickens, Charles, Introduction (1866), *Legends and Lyrics Together with a Chaplet of Verses* (London: George Bell and Sons, 1877), xi–xxxi.

Forster, Margaret, *Significant Sisters: The Grassroots of Active Feminism 1839–1939* (London: Secker and Warburg, 1984).

Gill, Gregory, *The Life and Work of Adelaide Procter: Poetry, Feminism and Fathers* (Aldershot: Ashgate, 1998).

Hirsch, Pam, *Barbara Leigh Smith Bodichon: Feminist, Artist and Rebel* (London: Pimlico, 1999).

Lacey, Candida Ann (ed.), *Barbara Leigh Smith Bodichon and the Langham Place Group*, (London and New York: Routledge, 1987).

Lohrli, Anne, *Household Words: A Weekly Journal 1850–1859 conducted by Charles Dickens, Table of Contents, List of Contributors and their Contributions based on the Household Words Office Book in the Morris L. Parrish Collection of Victorian Novelists, Princeton University Library* (Toronto: University of Toronto Press, 1973).

Maison, Margaret, 'Queen Victoria's Favourite Poet', *Listener and BBC Television Review*, 29 April 1965, 636–7.

Rendall, Jane, *Equal or Different: Women's Politics 1800–1914*, ed. Jane Rendall (Oxford: Basil Blackwell, 1987).

Thompson, Nichola Diane (ed.), *Victorian Women Writers and the Woman Question* (Cambridge: Cambridge University Press, 1999).

GENERAL READING

Primary

Barbauld, Anna, 'Thoughts on the Devotional Taste, On Sects, and on Establishments' (1775), in *Anna Letitia Barbauld: Selected Poetry and Prose*, ed. William McCarthy and Elizabeth Kraft (Ontario: Broadview, 2002), 209–34.

Browning, Elizabeth Barrett, *The Greek Christian Poets and the English Poets* (London: Chapman and Hall, 1863).

Coleridge, H. N., 'Modern English Poetesses', *Quarterly Review*, 66 (1840), 374–418.

Coleridge, Samuel Taylor, *Table Talk* (1836), ed. Carl Woodring, 2 vols (Princeton: Princeton University Press, 1990).

Goethe, Johann Wolfgang von, *Faust: Parts One and Two* (1808/1832; Indianapolis: Bobbs-Merrill, 1965).

Keble, John, *Lectures on Poetry 1832–1841*, trans. Edward Kershaw Francis (1844; Oxford: Clarendon Press, 1912).

Lockhart, John G., 'On the Cockney School of Poetry', *Blackwood's Edinburgh Magazine*, 2 (1817), 38–41.

Mill, John Stuart, 'What is Poetry' (1833), in F. Parvin Sharples (ed.), *Essays on Poetry*, (Columbia: University of South Carolina Press, 1976), 3–22.

Robinson, Mary, *Sappho and Phaon* (1796; Otley: Woodstock Books, 2000).

Schiller, Friedrich, *Essays Aesthetical and Philosophical* (London: George Bell and Sons, 1900).

Schiller, Friedrich, *The Poems of Schiller*, trans. E. A. Bowring (London: George Bell, 1882).

Shelley, Percy Bysshe, 'Defence of Poetry' (1821), in *Shelley's Poetry and Prose*, ed. Donald H. Reiman and Sharon B. Powers (London and New York: Norton, 1977), 480–508.

Staël, Madame de, *Corinne, or Italy*, trans. Sylvia Raphael (1807; Oxford: Oxford University Press, 1998).

Staël, Madame de, *A Treatise on the Influence of the Passions upon the Happiness of Individuals and of Nations* (London: George Cawthorn, 1798).

Young, Edward, *The Complete Works: Poetry and Prose*, 2 vols (London, 1854).

Wordsworth, William, 'Preface to *Lyrical Ballads, with Pastoral and Other Poems* (1802)', in *William Wordsworth: The Poems*, ed. John O. Hayden, 2 vols (London: Penguin, 1977), vol. 1, 867–96.

Criticism

Armstrong, Isobel, 'The Gush of the Feminine: How Can We Read Women's Poetry of the Romantic Period', in Paula R. Feldman and Theresa M. Kelley, *Romantic Women Writers: Voices and Countervoices* (Hanover and London: University Press of New England, 1995), 13–32.

Armstrong, Isobel, *The Radical Aesthetic* (Oxford: Blackwell, 2000).

Armstrong, Isobel, *Victorian Poetry: Poetry, Poetics and Politics* (London: Routledge, 1993).

Armstrong, Isobel, 'When Is a Victorian Poet Not a Victorian Poet? Poetry and the Politics of Subjectivity in the Long Nineteenth Century', *Victorian Studies*, 43:2 (2001), 279–92.

Armstrong, Isobel (ed.), *Women's Poetry in the Enlightenment: The Making of a Canon 1730–1820* (London: Macmillan, 1998).

Armstrong, Isobel (ed.), *Women's Poetry: Late Romantic to Late Victorian: Gender and Genre 1830–1900* (London: Macmillan, 1999).

Armstrong, Isobel, Joseph Bristow and Cath Sharrock (ed.), *Nineteenth-Century Women Poets: An Oxford Anthology* (Oxford: Clarendon Press, 1996).

Benson, Louis F., *The English Hymn: Its Development and Use in Worship* (London: Hodder and Stoughton, 1915).

Blank, G. Kim, *Wordsworth and Feeling: The Poetry of an Adult Child* (London: Associated University Presses, 1995).

Bristow, Joseph (ed.), *The Cambridge Companion to Victorian Poetry* (Cambridge: Cambridge University Press, 2000).

Canuel, Mark, *Religion, Toleration and British Writing 1790–1830* (Cambridge: Cambridge University Press, 2002).

Cronin, Richard, *Romantic Victorians: English Literature 1824–1840* (Basingstoke: Palgrave, 2002).

Davies, Horton, *Worship and Theology in England: From Watts and Wesley to Martineau 1690–1900* (Michigan: Eerdmans, 1996).

Greer, Germaine, *Slip-Shod Sibyls: Recognition, Rejection and the Woman Poet* (London: Viking, 1995).

Hardy, Barbara, *The Advantage of Lyric: Essays on Feeling in Poetry* (London: Athlone Press, 1977).

Homans, Margaret, *Bearing the Word: Language and Female Experience in Nineteenth-Century Women's Writing* (Chicago and London: University of Chicago Press, 1986).

Jackson, Virginia and Yopie Prins, 'Lyrical Studies', *Victorian Literature and Culture*, 27:2 (1999), 521–30.

Johnson, Dale A. (ed.), *Studies in Women and Religion 10: Women in English Religion* (New York and Toronto: Edwin Mellen Press, 1983).

Leighton, Angela, and Margaret Reynolds (eds), *Victorian Women Poets: An Anthology*, (Oxford: Blackwell, 1995).

Leader, Zachary, and Ian Haywood (eds), *Romantic Period Writings 1798–1832: An Anthology* (London: Routledge, 1998).

McGann, Jerome, *The Poetics of Sensibility: A Revolution in Literary Style* (Oxford: Clarendon Press, 1996).

Maxwell, Catherine, *The Female Sublime from Milton to Swinburne: Bearing Blindness* (Manchester: Manchester University Press, 2001).

Maynard, John, *Victorian Discourses on Sexuality and Religion* (Cambridge: Cambridge University Press, 1993).

Mee, Jon, *Romanticism, Enthusiasm, and Regulation: Poetics and the Policing of Culture in the Romantic Period* (Oxford: Oxford University Press, 2003).

Mellor, Anne K., *Mothers of the Nation: Women's Political Writing in England 1780–1830* (Indianapolis: Indiana University Press, 2000).

Melnyk, Julie (ed.), *Women's Theology in Nineteenth-Century Britain: Transfiguring the Faith of their Fathers* (New York and London: Garland Publishing Inc., 1998).

Scheinberg, Cynthia, *Women's Poetry and Religion in Victorian England: Jewish Identity and Christian Culture* (Cambridge: Cambridge University Press, 2002).

Shattock, Joanne (ed.), *Women and Literature in Britain, 1800–1900* (Cambridge: Cambridge University Press, 2001).

Soloman, Robert, *The Passions: Emotions and the Meaning of Life* (Indianapolis: Hackett Publishing, 1993).

Index